JAMMU & KASHMIR

A STATE STUDY GUIDE

MAJID KHAN

Published by

Hawk Press
4836/24, Ansari Road, Daryaganj
New Delhi – 110 002
Phones: 91-11-23278618, 91-11-43667199
E-mail: thehawkpress@gmail.com
www.thehawkpress.com

ISBN: 978-93-88318-76-1

Preface

Jammu and Kashmir is a state in northern India, often denoted by its acronym, J&K. It is located mostly in the Himalayan mountains, and shares borders with the states of Himachal Pradesh and Punjabto the south. The Line of Control separates it from the Pakistani-administered territories of Azad Kashmir and Gilgit-Baltistan in the west and north respectively, and a Line of Actual Control separates it from the Chinese-administered territory of Aksai Chin in the east. The state has special autonomy under Article 370 of the Constitution of India.

The picturesque valley of Kashmir situated on the northern extremity of India, occupies a position of unique and strategic importance in the sub-continent of India. It excels in beauty, art, architecture, culture and tradition, rivers, mountains, flora and fauna than several regions of the world. So far so, some eminent writers have compared this Himalayan range with that of Switzerland. Whereas, Kashmir bore the pangs of various onslaughts from North-West, Switzerland enjoyed peaceful postures for centuries.

A part of the former Princely State of Kashmir and Jammu, the region is the subject of a territorial conflict among China, India and Pakistan. The western districts of the former princely state known as Azad Kashmir and the northern territories known as Gilgit-Baltistan have been under Pakistani control since 1947. The Aksai Chin region in the east, bordering Tibet, has been under Chinese control since 1962.

Jammu and Kashmir consist of three regions: Jammu, the

Kashmir Valley and Ladakh. Srinagar is the summer capital, and Jammuis the winter capital. Jammu and Kashmir is the only state in India with a Muslim-majority population. The Kashmir valley is famous for its beautiful mountainous landscape, and Jammu's numerous shrines attract tens of thousands of Hindu pilgrims every year, while Ladakh is renowned for its remote mountain beauty and Buddhist culture.

Jammu and Kashmir is the only state in India which enjoys special autonomy under Article 370 of the Constitution of India, according to which no law enacted by the Parliament of India, except for those in the field of defence, communication and foreign policy, will be extendable in Jammu and Kashmir unless it is ratified by the state legislature of Jammu and Kashmir. Subsequently, jurisdiction of the Supreme Court of India over Jammu and Kashmir has been extended.

This is a reference book. All the matter is just compiled and edited in nature, taken from the various sources which are in public domain.

This book will prove useful and informative to the planners, policy makers in the government and to social researchers, students in academics.

—Editor

ABOUT THE BOOK

All the three regions of Jammu and Kashmir state viz., Jammu, Kashmir and Ladakh have contributed significantly to the development of the state. But due to lack of data no concerted efforts were made to analyse the role of different sectors in the development of the state economy. Jammu and Kashmir is a state in northern India, often denoted by its acronym, J&K. It is located mostly in the Himalayan mountains, and shares borders with the states of Himachal Pradesh and Punjabto the south. The Line of Control separates it from the Pakistani-administered territories of Azad Kashmir and Gilgit-Baltistan in the west and north respectively, and a Line of Actual Control separates it from the Chinese-administered territory of Aksai Chin in the east. The state has special autonomy under Article 370 of the Constitution of India. From Jammu and Kashmir's accession to India in 1947 to the various negotiations thereafter; Sheikh Abdullah's arrest to the framing of the Constitution of Jammu and Kashmir and the replacement of Sadar-i-Riyasat, this book impeccably documents the little-known constitutional history of the state. The picturesque valley of Kashmir situated on the northern extremity of India, occupies a position of unique and strategic importance in the sub-continent of India. It excels in beauty, art, architecture, culture and tradition, rivers, mountains, flora and fauna than several regions of the world.This book will prove useful and informative to the planners, policy makers in the government and to social researchers, students in academics.

Contents

	Preface	*(iii)*
1.	State at a Glance	1
2.	Culture and Society	11
3.	Government and Politics	32
4.	Language and Literature	56
5.	Geography and Flora & Fauna	79
6.	Economy	115
7.	Tourism	153
8.	Population and Religion	179
9.	Art, Architecture, Fair and Festivals	187
10.	Education	197
	Bibliography	205
	Index	207

1

State at a Glance

Jammu and Kashmir is a state in northern India, often denoted by its acronym, J&K. It is located mostly in the Himalayan mountains, and shares borders with the states of Himachal Pradesh and Punjab to the south. The Line of Control separates it from the Pakistani-administered territories of Azad Kashmir and Gilgit-Baltistan in the west and north respectively, and a Line of Actual Control separates it from the Chinese-administered territory of Aksai Chin in the east. The state has special autonomy under Article 370 of the Constitution of India.

A part of the former Princely State of Kashmir and Jammu, the region is the subject of a territorial conflict among China, India and Pakistan. The western districts of the former princely state known as Azad Kashmir and the northern territories known as Gilgit-Baltistan have been under Pakistani control since 1947. The Aksai Chin region in the east, bordering Tibet, has been under Chinese control since 1962.

Jammu and Kashmir consist of three regions: Jammu, the Kashmir Valley and Ladakh. Srinagar is the summer capital, and Jammu is the winter capital. Jammu and Kashmir is the only state in India with a Muslim-majority population. The Kashmir valley is famous for its beautiful mountainous landscape, and Jammu's numerous shrines attract tens of thousands of Hindu pilgrims every year, while Ladakh is renowned for its remote mountain beauty and Buddhist culture.

HISTORY

Accession

Maharaja of Kashmir, Hari Singh (1895–1961)

The Instrument of Accession of Kashmir to India was accepted by Governor General Louis Mountbatten, 1st Earl Mountbatten of Burma.

Maharaja Hari Singh became the ruler of the princely state of Jammu and Kashmir in 1925, and he was the reigning monarch at the conclusion of the British rule in the subcontinent in 1947. With the impending independence of India, the British announced that the British Paramountcy over the princely states would end, and the states were free to choose between the new Dominions of India and Pakistan or to remain independent. It was emphasized that independence was only a 'theoretical possibility' because, during the long rule of the British in India, the states had come to depend on British Indian government for a variety of their needs including their internal and external security.

Jammu and Kashmir had a Muslim majority (77% Muslim by the previous census in 1941). Following the logic of Partition, many people in Pakistan expected that Kashmir would join Pakistan. However, the predominant political movement in the Valley of Kashmir (Jammu and Kashmir National Conference) was secular and was allied with the Indian National Congress since the 1930s. So many in India too had expectations that Kashmir would join India. The Maharaja was faced with indecision.

On 22 October 1947, rebellious citizens from the western districts of the State and Pushtoon tribesmen from the Northwest Frontier Province of Pakistan invaded the State, backed by Pakistan. The Maharaja initially fought back but appealed for assistance to the India, who agreed on the condition that the ruler accede to India. Maharaja Hari Singh signed the Instrument of Accession on 26 October 1947 in return for military aid and assistance, which was accepted by the Governor General the next day. While the Government of India accepted the accession, it added the proviso that it would be submitted to a "reference to the people" after the state is cleared of the invaders, since "only the people, not the Maharaja, could decide where Kashmiris wanted to live." It was a provisional accession.

Once the Instrument of Accession was signed, Indian soldiers entered Kashmir with orders to evict the raiders. The resulting Indo-Pakistani War of 1947 lasted till the end of 1948. At the beginning of 1948, India took the matter to the United Nations Security Council. The Security Council passed a resolution asking Pakistan to withdraw its forces as well as the Pakistani nationals from the territory of Jammu and Kashmir, and India to withdraw the majority of its forces leaving only a sufficient number to maintain law and order, following which a Plebiscite would be held. A ceasefire was agreed on 1 January 1949, supervised by UN observers.

A special United Nations Commission for India and Pakistan (UNCIP) was set up to negotiate the withdrawal arrangements as per the Security Council resolution. The UNCIP made three visits to the subcontinent between 1948 and 1949, trying to find a solution agreeable to both India and Pakistan. It passed a resolution in August 1948 proposing a three-part process. It was accepted by India but effectively rejected by Pakistan. In the end, no withdrawal was ever carried out, India insisting that Pakistan had to withdraw first, and Pakistan contending that there was no guarantee that India would withdraw afterward. No agreement could be reached between the two countries on the process of demilitarization.

India and Pakistan fought two further wars in 1965 and 1971. Following the latter war, the countries reached the Simla Agreement, agreeing on a Line of Control between their respective regions and committing to a peaceful resolution of the dispute through bilateral negotiations.

MUSLIM RULE

In the 13th century, Islam first became the dominant religion in Kashmir. The Muslims and Hindus of Kashmir lived in relative harmony, since the Sufi-Islamic way of life that ordinary Muslims followed in Kashmir complemented the Rishi tradition of Kashmiri Pandits. This led to a syncretic culture where Hindus and Muslims revered the same local saints and prayed at the same shrines. Famous sufi saint Bulbul Shah was able to persuade the king of the time Rinchan Shah who was prince of Kashgar Laddakh, through his intellectual power to adopt Islamic way of life and the foundation of Sufiana composite culture was laid when Muslims, Hindus and Buddhists were co-existing in the atmosphere of love and brotherhood.

Some Kashmiri rulers, such as Sultan Zain-ul-Abidin, were tolerant of all religions in a manner comparable to Akbar. However, several Muslim rulers of Kashmir were intolerant to other religions. Sultan Sikandar Butshikan of Kashmir (AD 1389-1413) is often considered the worst of these. Historians have recorded many of his atrocities. The Tarikh-i-Firishta records that Sikandar persecuted the Hindus and issued orders proscribing the residence of any other than Muslims in Kashmir. He also ordered the breaking of all "golden and silver images".

The Tarikh-i-Firishta further states: "Many of the Brahmins, rather than abandon their religion or their country, poisoned themselves; some emigrated from their native homes, while a few escaped the evil of banishment by becoming Mohammedans. After the emigration of the Brahmins, Sikandar ordered all the temples in Kashmir to be thrown down......Having broken all the images in Kashmir, (Sikandar) acquired the title of 'Destroyer of Idols'."

The Histories: The metrical chronicle of the kings of Kashmir, called *Rajatarangini,* has been pronounced by Professor H.I.Wilson to be the only Sanskrit composition yet discovered to which the appellation "history" can with any propriety be applied. It first became known to the Muslims when, on Akbar's invasion of Kashmir in 1588, a copy was presented to the emperor. A translation into Persian was made at his order. A summary of its contents, taken from this Persian translation, is given by Abul Fazl in the *Ain-i-Akbari.* The *Rajatarangini* was written by Kalhana about the middle of the 12th century. His work, in six books, makes use of earlier writings that are now lost.

The *Rajatarangini* is the first of a series of four histories that record the annals of Kashmir. Commencing with a rendition of traditional history of very early times, the *Rajatarangini* comes down to the reign of Sangrama Deva, (*c.*1006 AD). The second work, by Jonaraja, continues the history from where

Kalhana left off, and, entering the Muslim period, gives an account of the reigns down to that of Zain-ul-ab-ad-din, 1412. P. Srivara carried on the record to the accession of Fah Shah in 1486. The fourth work, called *Rajavalipataka,* by Prajnia Bhatta, completes the history to the time of the incorporation of Kashmir in the dominions of the Mogul emperor Akbar, 1588.

Princely State of Kashmir and Jammu: By the early 19th century, the Kashmir valley had passed from the control of the Durrani Empire of Afghanistan, and four centuries of Muslim rule under the Mughals and the Afghans, to the conquering Sikh armies. Earlier, in 1780, after the death of Ranjit Deo, the Raja of Jammu, the kingdom of Jammu (to the south of the Kashmir valley) was captured by the Sikhs under Ranjit Singh of Lahore and afterwards, until 1846, became a tributary to the Sikh power.

Ranjit Deo's grand-nephew, Gulab Singh, subsequently sought service at the court of Ranjit Singh, distinguished himself in later campaigns, especially the annexation of the Kashmir valley by the Sikhs army in 1819, and, for his services, was created Raja of Jammu in 1820. With the help of his officer, Zorawar Singh, Gulab Singh soon captured Laddakh and Baltistan, regions to the east and northeast of Jammu.

In 1845, the First Anglo-Sikh War broke out, and Gulab Singh "contrived to hold himself aloof till the battle of Sobraon (1846), when he appeared as a useful mediator and the trusted advisor of Sir Henry Lawrence. Two treaties were concluded.

By the first the State of Lahore (*i.e.* West Punjab) handed over to the British, as equivalent for (rupees) one crore of indemnity, the hill countries between Beas and Indus; by the second the British made over to Gulab Singh for (Rupees) 75 lakhs all the hilly or mountainous country situated to the east of Indus and west of Ravi" (*i.e.* the Vale of Kashmir). Soon after Gulab Singh's death in 1857, his son, Ranbir Singh, added the emirates of Hunza, Gilgit and Nagar to the kingdom.

The *Princely State of Kashmir and Jammu* (as it was then called) was constituted between 1820 and 1858 and was "somewhat artificial in composition and it did not develop a fully coherent identity, partly as a result of its disparate origins and partly as a result of the autocratic rule which it experienced on the fringes of Empire."

It combined disparate regions, religions, and ethnicities: to the east, Laddakh was ethnically and culturally Tibetan and its inhabitants practised Buddhism; to the south, Jammu had a mixed population of Hindus, Muslims and Sikhs; in the heavily populated central Kashmir valley, the population was overwhelmingly *Sunni* Muslim, however, there was also a small but influential Hindu minority, the Kashmiri Brahmins or pandits; to the northeast, sparsely populated Baltistan had a population ethnically related to Laddakh, but which practised *Shia* Islam; to the north, also sparsely populated, Gilgit Agency, was an area of diverse, mostly *Shia* groups; and, to the west, Punch was Muslim, but of different ethnicity than the Kashmir valley.

After the Indian Rebellion of 1857, in which Kashmir sided with the British, and the subsequent assumption of direct rule by Great Britain, the princely state of Kashmir came under the paramountcy of the British Crown.

1947

Ranbir Singh's grandson Hari Singh, who had ascended the throne of Kashmir in 1925, was the reigning monarch in 1947 at the conclusion of British rule of the subcontinent and the subsequent partition of the British Indian Empire into the newly independent Union of India and the Dominion of Pakistan.

As parties to the partition process, both countries had agreed that the rulers of princely states would be given the right to opt for either Pakistan or India or—in special cases—to remain independent. In 1947, Kashmir's population "was 77 per cent Muslim and it shared a boundary with Pakistan. Hence, it was anticipated that the Maharaja would accede to Pakistan, when the British paramountcy ended on 14-15 August."

To postpone making a hurried decision, the Maharaja signed

a "standstill" agreement with Pakistan, which ensured continuity of trade, travel, communication, and similar services between the two. India did not sign a similar agreement. Meanwhile, Indian postal services began listing Kashmir as Indian territory, causing alarm in Pakistan.

In October 1947, Pashtuns from Pakistan's North-West Frontier Province invaded Kashmir in support of a rebellion against the Maharaja which had erupted in the restive Poonch district. The ostensible aim of the guerrilla campaign was to frighten Hari Singh into submission. "Instead the Maharaja appealed to Mountbatten for assistance, and the Governor-General agreed on the condition that the ruler accede to India."

Once the Maharaja signed the Instrument of Accession, "Indian soldiers entered Kashmir and drove the Pakistani-sponsored irregulars from all but a small section of the state. The United Nations was then invited to mediate the quarrel. The UN mission insisted that the opinion of Kashmiris must be ascertained, while India insisted that no referandum could occur until all of the state had been cleared of irregulars."

The Pakistani government immediately contested the accession, suggesting that it was fraudulent, that the Maharaja acted under duress, and that he had no right to sign an agreement with India when the standstill agreement with Pakistan was still in force.

POST-1947

In the last days of 1948, a ceasefire was agreed under UN auspices; however, since the plebiscite demanded by the UN was never conducted, relations between India and Pakistan soured, and eventually led to two more wars over Kashmir in 1965 and 1999. India has control of about half the area of the former princely state of Jammu and Kashmir; Pakistan controls a third of the region, the Northern Areas and Pakistan Occupied Kashmir.

According to Encyclopaedia Britannica, "Although there was a clear Muslim majority in Kashmir before the 1947 partition and its economic, cultural, and geographic contiguity with the Muslim-majority area of the Punjab (in Pakistan) could be convincingly demonstrated, the political developments during and after the partition resulted in a division of the region. Pakistan was left with territory that, although basically Muslim in character, was thinly populated, relatively inaccessible, and economically underdeveloped.

The largest Muslim group, situated in the Vale of Kashmir and estimated to number more than half the population of the entire region, lay in Indian-administered territory, with its former outlets via the Jhelum valley route blocked."

The UN Security Council on 20 January 1948 passed Resolution 39, establishing a special commission to investigate the conflict. Subsequent to the commission's recommendation, the Security Council ordered in its Resolution 47, passed on 21 April 1948, that the invading Pakistani army retreat from Jammu & Kashmir and that the accession of Kashmir to either India or Pakistan be determined in accordance with a plebiscite to be supervised by the UN.

In a string of subsequent resolutions, the Security Council took notice of the continuing failure to hold the plebiscite.

The Government of India holds that the Maharaja signed a document of accession to India October 26, 1947. Pakistan has disputed whether the Maharaja actually signed the accession treaty before Indian troops entered Kashmir. Furthermore, Pakistan claims the Indian government has never produced an original copy of this accession treaty and thus its validity and legality is disputed. Alan Campbell-Johnson, the press attache to the Viceroy of India states that "The legality of the accession is beyond doubt."

The eastern region of the erstwhile princely state of Kashmir has also been beset with a boundary dispute. In the late 19th- and early 20th centuries, although some boundary agreements were signed between Great Britain, Afghanistan and Russia over the northern borders of Kashmir, China never accepted these agreements, and the official Chinese position did not change with the communist takeover in 1949.

By the mid-1950s the Chinese army had entered the northeast portion of Laddakh. : "By 1956–57 they had completed a military road through the Aksai Chin area to provide better communication between Xinjiang and western Tibet. India's belated discovery of this road led to border clashes between the two countries that culminated in the Sino-Indian war of October 1962." China has occupied Aksai Chin since 1962 and, in addition, an adjoining region, the Trans-Karakoram Tract was ceded by Pakistan to China in 1965.

In 1949, the Indian government obliged Hari Singh to leave Jammu and Kashmir, and yield the government to Sheikh Abdullah, the leader of a popular political party, the National Conference Party. Since then, a bitter enmity has been developed between India and Pakistan and three wars have taken place between them over Kashmir.

The growing dispute over Kashmir also lead to the rise of militancy in the state. The year 1989 saw the intensification of conflict in Jammu and Kashmir as Mujahadeens from Afghanistan slowly infiltrated the region following the end of the Soviet-Afghan War the same year.

2

Culture and Society

CULTURE

Buddhism is an integral part of Ladakh's culture. Shown here is a statue of Buddha in a monastery in Likir.

Ladakh is famous for its unique Indo-Tibetan culture. Chanting in Sanskrit and Tibetan language forms an integral part of Ladakh's Buddhist lifestyle. Annual masked dance festivals, weaving and archery are an important part of traditional life in Ladakh. Ladakhi food has much in common with Tibetan food, the most prominent foods being thukpa, noodle soup; and tsampa, known in Ladakhi as *Ngampe*, roasted barley flour. Typical garb includes gonchas of velvet, elaborately embroidered waistcoats and boots, and gonads or hats. People adorned with gold and silver ornaments and turquoise headgears throng the streets during Ladakhi festivals.

The *Dumhal* is a famous dance in the Kashmir Valley, performed by men of the Wattal region. The women perform the Rouff, another traditional folk dance. Kashmir has been noted for its fine arts for centuries, including poetry and handicrafts. *Shikaras*, traditional small wooden boats, and houseboats are a common feature in lakes and rivers across the Valley.

Due to the special status the State enjoys in the Indian Union, people from outside the state cannot purchase land in the state. As a consequence, houseboats became popular among those who were unable to purchase land in the Valley and have now become an integral part of the Kashmiri lifestyle.

Kehwa, traditional green tea with spices and almond, is consumed all through the day in the chilly winter climate of Kashmir. Most of the buildings in the Valley and Ladakh are made from softwood and are influenced by Indian, Tibetan, and Islamic architecture.

Jammu's Dogra culture and tradition is very similar to that of neighboring Punjab and Himachal Pradesh. Traditional Punjabi festivals such as Lohri and Vaisakhi are celebrated with great zeal and enthusiasm throughout the region, along with Accession Day, an annual holiday which commemorates the accession of Jammu & Kashmir to the Dominion of India. After *Dogras*, *Gujjars* form the second-largest ethnic group in Jammu. Known for their semi-nomadic lifestyle, Gujjars are also found in large numbers in the Kashmir Valley. Similar to Gujjars, *Gaddis* are primarily herdsmen who hail from the Chamba region in Himachal Pradesh. Gaddis is generally associated with emotive music played on the flute. The *Bakkarwalas* found both in Jammu and the Kashmir valley is wholly nomadic pastoral people who move along the Himalayan slopes in search of pastures for their huge flocks of goats and sheep. The Shri Pratap Singh Museum in Srinagar is the main repository of Kashmiri elite culture and royal heritage. The Meeras Mahal in Noor Bagh, near Sopore, founded by Atiqa Bano, holds the material and artistic heritage of the common folk.

CULTURE OF KASHMIR

The culture of Kashmir refers to the culture and traditions of Kashmir, a region in northern India (consisting of Jammu and Kashmir), northeast Pakistan (consisting of Azad Kashmir and Gilgit–Baltistan) and the Chinese Occupied territory of Aksai Chin.

The culture of Kashmir is a diverse blend and highly influenced by northern South Asian, Persian as well as Central Asian culture. Along with its scenic beauty, Kashmir is famous for its cultural heritage; it amalgamates Muslim, Hindu, Sikh and Buddhist philosophies and has involved composite culture based on the values of humanism and tolerance which is collectively known as *Kashmiriyat*. Jammu, Kashmir and Ladakh each have their own distinct culture.

Background

Kashmir

One of the most important parts of the cultural identity of the Kashmiri people is the Kashmiri (Koshur) language. This language is spoken only in the Valley of Kashmir by the Kashmiri Pandits and Kashmiri Muslims. Besides language, Wazwan and culture has been greatly influenced by Central Asian and Persian culture. Kashmiri is an Indo-Aryan (Dardic subgroup) language close to Central Asian Avestan-Persian. Cultural music and dance like *Wanvun*, *Roaff*, carpet/shawl weaving | Kaleenbafi and *Koshur Sufiana* forms a very important part of Kashmiri identity. Kashmir has witnessed many spiritual gurus who migrated from their land to Kashmir. Kashmir has also even witnessed the birth of some of the great poets and suifs of all time like *Lal Daed, Sheikh-ul-Alam*, Habba Khatoon and many more; and is regarded as Peer Vaer (a place or land of spiritual gurus). It is important to note that Kashmiri culture is predominantly followed only in the Kashmir valley and Doda of the Chenab region. Jammu and Ladakh have their own distinct cultures that are very different from that of Kashmir.

The *Dumhal* is a famous dance in the Kashmir valley, performed by men of the Wattal region. The women perform the Roaff, another traditional folk dance. Kashmir has been noted for its fine arts for centuries, including poetry and handicrafts. *Shikaras*, traditional small wooden boats, and houseboatsare a common feature in various lakes and rivers across the Valley. Kashmiri culture is defined in terms of religious values, Kashmiri language, literature, cuisine and traditional values of mutual respect. The overwhelming majority of Kashmiris are Muslims and Islamic identity plays a very important role in the daily lives of people. Kashmiris across the religious divide have for centuries shared cordial and friendly ties. Kashmiri poets and writers like Mehjoor, Abdul Ahad Azad, etc. enriched the literature with their poetry. Kashmiri cuisine holds a unique place among different world cuisines. Salted tea or Noon Chai also called Sheer Chai is the traditional drink and is cooked in a Samavar, a Kashmiri tea-pot. Kashmir has been noted for its fine arts for centuries, including poetry and handicrafts. *Shikaras*, traditional small wooden boats, and houseboats are a common feature in various lakes and rivers across the Valley. *Kehwa*, traditional green tea with spices like cardamom, Saffron and almond, is served on special occasions and festivals. Kashmiri weddings are regarded incomplete without the Kashmiri traditional food known as Wazwan, which is typically spicy food cooked by the traditional cooks (Waz). Wazwan is a multi-course meal in which almost all the dishes are meat-based.

Ladakh

Culture of Ladakh is famous for its unique Indo-Tibetan culture. Chanting in Sanskrit and Tibetan language forms an integral part of Ladakh's Buddhist lifestyle. Annual masked dance festivals, weaving and archery are an important part of traditional life in Ladakh. Ladakhi food has much in common with Tibetan food, the most prominent foods being thukpa, noodle soup; and tsampa, known in Ladakhi as *Ngampe*, roasted barley flour. Typical garb includes gonchas of velvet, elaborately embroidered waistcoats and boots, and gonads or hats. People, adorned with gold and silver ornaments and turquoise headgears throng the streets during various Ladakhi festivals.

Jammu

Jammu's Dogra culture and tradition is very different from the Kashmiri culture. The Dogra culture is instead much similar to that of neighbouring Punjab and Himachal Pradesh. Traditional Punjabi festivals such as Lohri and Baisakhi are celebrated with great zeal and enthusiasm throughout the region, along with Accession Day, an annual holiday which commemorates the accession of Jammu & Kashmir to the Dominion of India. After Dogras, *Gujjars* form the second-largest ethnic group in Jammu. Known for their semi-nomadic lifestyle, Gujjars are also found in large numbers in the Kashmir valley. Similar to Gujjars, *Gaddis* are primarily herdsmen who hail from the Chamba region in Himachal Pradesh. Gaddis are generally associated with emotive music played on the flute. The *Bakkarwalas* found both in Jammu and the outskirts of the Vale of Kashmir are wholly nomadic pastoral people who move along the Himalayan slopes in search for pastures for their huge flocks of goats and sheep.

Cuisine

Kashmir has a variety of meat based dishes like Rogan Josh, a lamb dish. Wazwan is a multi-course dish which is served on occasions like weddings.

Language and literature

The Kashmiri language is the main language spoken in Kashmir, although many other Indo-Aryan languages are also prevalent. Kashmiri literature has a rich history stretching back to hundreds of years.

CUISINES

In the olden times, almost every Kashmiri home in the plains had a professional Kashmiri cook in residences who were the masters of their art. Pure ghee and mustard oil was used freely and every mealtime was an event in itself. Gradually and with time, the ladies of the household learnt the art under the specialized training of these culinary masters and became as proficient as their 'gurus'. As the living costs increased with time, the era of the super cooks came to an end. However, their art has not all lost.

One can frequently taste the delicacies mastered by the chefs at Kashmiri weddings. Kashmiri cuisine that evolved in the Valley several centuries ago acquired some of the scrumptious elements of the Mughal art of cooking and yet has retained a distinct personality of its own. There were two great schools of culinary craftsmanship in Kashmir, namely those of Kashmiri Pandits and Kashmiri Muslims. The basic difference between the two schools was that the abundant use of heeng (asafetida) and curd among the Hindus and the open-handed use of onions and garlics among the Muslims.

Hindu Brahmins or *Kashmiri Pandits* are not averse to eating meat and are rather voracious meat eaters. However, they prefer goat and that too a young one. The meat is generally chosen from the legs, neck, breast, ribs and shoulders and cut into large pieces. No vegetarian or non-vegetarian dish, except certain kababs, is cooked without curd. The Kashmiris often cook their food by heating it on two sides, from both top and bottom for that distinctive taste. The charcoal fire was their solution in the earlier days but oven serves as a good substitute these days.

Originally, Kashmiri Pandits avoided onions and garlics but now many of them have acquired a taste for them and include them in certain recipes as optional. Though the basic principles of cooking are largely similar in almost all homes, certain Pandit families have adopted minor changes in both ingredients and methods. The most important of the retained traits are the liberal use of aromatic spices and the avoidance of onion and garlic in some homes. Kabargah, Kofta, Dum Alu, Methi Chaman and Firni are some of the delicacies of the region known for their sheer flavor and richness.

Kashmiri Muslims offer another gold mine of gourmet though except for the few restaurants and regional stalls in the country, this art is near extinction. Largely confined to Kashmiri homes in and out of the Valley, the professional cooks and masters of the art are known as 'wazas'. These people claim to be the descendants of the master chefs who migrated from Samarkand and parts of Central Asia at the beginning of the fifteenth century and were a vital part of the entourage that came to Kashmir during the reign of Timur (or Tamarlane).

In the earlier days, the traditional Kashmiri Muslim banquet known as Wazwan, a feast fit for kings, which was perhaps the most unique and elaborate royal spread of meat and delicacies compared to the other parts of India. Comprising of thirty-six courses, fifteen to thirty dishes of Wazwan are varieties of meat. Many of the delicacies are cooked through the entire night under the expert supervision of a Vasta Waza or head chef, assisted by an entourage of wazas under him. Kashmir's most formal meal, Wazwan is not only a ritual but also a ceremony. Traditionally, no spoons, forks or knives are used for eating food. Eaten with fingers, getting invited to a Wazwan is a rare luxury that one can enjoy these days.

HANDICRAFTS

Jammu and Kashmir is not only home to the vast cultural and ethnic diversity but also the myriad arts and crafts that have been carefully nurtured for the centuries. A variety of motifs, techniques and crafts flourished in the land as the people from different regions flocked through this beautiful place and many of the skilled craftsmen decided to settle amidst its charming abundance of natural beauty. With time, these arts have gained even more distinctiveness and today Kashmir is known for woollen textiles, Pashmina shawls, embroidered suits, Kashmir silk saris, papier mache, woodcarving, hand knotted carpets and lots of other traditional crafts.

Carpet: Kashmiri carpets are world renowned for two things - they are hand made and they are always knotted, never tufted. The yarn used normally is silk, wool or silk and wool. Woollen carpets always have a cotton base while silk usually have cotton base. Sometimes however, if the base is also in silk then the cost increases proportionately. Occasionally, carpets are made on a cotton base, mainly of woollen pile with silk yarn used as highlights on certain motifs. The soothing blend of colours makes the Kashmiri carpet a prized possession.

Carpet weaving in Kashmir was not originally indigenous but is thought to have come in by way of Persia. Till today most designs are distinctly Persian with local variations. One example, however, of a typical Kashmiri design is the tree of life. The colours of Kashmiri carpets are more subtle and muted than elsewhere in the country. The knotting of the carpet is the most important aspect, determining its durability and value, in addition to its design. Basically, the more knots per square inch, the greater its value and durability. Also there are single and double-knotted carpets. A single knotted carpet is fluffier and more resistant to touch.

Namdas: Far less expensive are these colorful floor coverings made from woollen and cotton fiber, which has been manually pressed into shape. Prices vary with the percentage of wool—a Namda containing 80% wool being more expensive than one containing 20% wool. Chain stitch embroidery in woollen and cotton thread is worked on these rugs.

Papier Mache: Besides at least three different grades of Papier Mache, there are some cheaper versions in cardboard or wood available too. To make Papier Mache, first paper is soaked in water till it disintegrates. It is then pounded, mixed with an adhesive solution, shaped over moulds, and allowed to dry and set before being painted and varnished. Paper that has been pounded to pulp has the smoothest finish in the final product. The designs painted on objects of Papier Mache are brightly coloured. They vary in artistry and the choices of colours. Gold is used on most objects, either as the only colour, or as the highlight for certain motifs, and besides the finish of the product, it is the quality of the gold used which determines the price.

Pure Gold leaf, which has the unmistakable luster, is far more expensive than bronze dust or gold poster paint but also has much longer life and will never fade or tarnish. Varnish, which is applied to the finished product, imparts a high gloss and smoothness, which increases with every coat. Cardboard, usually indistinguishable from Papier Mache, gives slightly when pressed firmly.

Shawls: There are three fibers from which the Kashmiri shawls are made - Wool, Pashmina and Shahtoosh. Woollen shawls being are the cheapest while the Shahtoosh are the most expensive ones. Woollen shawls are popular because of the embroidery, worked on them, which is a specialty to Kashmir. Both embroidery and the type of wool used causes differences in price.

Many kinds of embroidery are worked on shawls - 'sozni' or needlework is generally done in a panel along the sides of the shawl. Motifs, usually abstract designs or stylized paisleys and flowers are worked in one or two, occasionally three colours, all subdued. Another type of needle embroidery is popularly known as Papier Mache work because of the design and the style in which it is executed. This is done either in broad panels or either side of the breadth of a shawl, or covering the entire surface of a shawl. Ari or hook embroidery; motifs are well-known flower design finely worked in concentric rings of chain stitch.

Pashmina shawls are unmistakably soft and its yarn is spun from the hair of the ibex found at 14,000 ft. above the sea level. Although pure Pashmina is expensive, sometimes blending it with rabbit fur or with wool brings down the cost. Shahtoosh is the legendary 'ring shawl', renowned for its lightness, softness and warmth. The astronomical price it commands in the market is due to the scarcity of raw material.

High in the plateaux of Tibet and the eastern part of Laddakh, at an altitude of above 5,000 meters, roam Pantholops Hodgosoni or Tibetan antelope. During grazing, a few strands of the downy hair from the throat are shed and it is these, which are painstakingly collected until there are enough for a shawl.

Yarn is spun either from Shahtoosh alone, or with Pashmina to bring down the cost. In the case of pure Shahtoosh too, there are many qualities - the yarn can be spun so skillfully as to resemble a strand of silk. Not only are shawls made from such fine yarn extremely expensive, they can only be loosely woven and are too flimsy for embroidery to be done on them. Unlike woollen or Pashmina shawls, Shahtoosh is seldom dyed. Its natural colour is mousy brown, and it is, at the most, sparsely embroidered.

Chain Stitch and Crewel Furnishings: Chain stitch, be it in wool, silk or cotton, is done by hook rather than any needle. Because of the high quality of embroidery done on wall hangings and rugs, Kashmiri crewelwork is in great demand all over the world. All the embroidery is executed on white cotton fabric, pre-shrunk by the manufacturers. The intrinsic worth of each piece lies in the size of the stitches and the yarn used.

Saffron, Walnuts, Almonds, Honey: Pampore, outside Srinagar, is the only place in the world besides Spain where saffron is grown. It is the most expensive spice in the world. Sealed jars of this Spice, with the Government laboratory's stamp approval, are available all over Srinagar. The climate of Kashmir is ideal for walnut and almond trees, which grow here in abundance. Natural honey too, is a produce of the apiaries, which abound in the state.

Silks, Tweeds: Tweed is woven in Kashmir with pure, never blended, wool. The resultant fabric competes favourably with the best fabric in the world. Sericulture is another important industry of the state. The cocoon reared in Kashmir is of the superior quality, yielding an extremely fine fiber, and any silk woven from this thread becomes known. The fineness of the yarn lends itself particularly well to the weaves known as 'chinon' and 'crepe de chine', in addition to the universally recognized silk weave. Interestingly, just as little or no raw material for tweed comes from Kashmir, almost no weaving and printing of silk is done in the state.

Pherans: This garment seems to be fusion of a coat and a cloak and is loose enough to admit the inevitable brazier of live coals, which is carried around in much the same way as a hot water bottle. Men's pherans are always made of tweed or coarse wool while women's pherans, somewhat more stylized, are most commonly made of raffel with splashes of ari or hook embroidery at the throat, cuffs and edges. The quality of embroidery and thickness of the raffel determines the price.

Basketry: Willow rushes that grow profusely in marshes and lakes of Kashmir are used to make charmingly attractive objects such as shopping baskets, lampshades, tables and chairs and are generally inexpensive. To increase their life span, unvarnished products should be chiselled and frequently sprayed with water, particularly in hot, dry climates, to prevent them from being brittle.

Walnut Wood: Kashmir is the only part of India where the walnut tree grows. Its colour, grains and inherent sheen are unique and unmistakable, and the carving and fret work that is done on this wood is of a very superior quality. There are two types of walnut trees—the fruit bearing species whose wood is so well known, and one that bears no fruit and is locally known as 'zangul'. Zangul has none of the beauty of walnut wood, being much less strong and possessing no grain while the walnut wood is almost black and its grains are much more pronounced than the wood of the trunk, which is lighter in colour. The branches have the lightest colour, being almost blonde and have no noticeable grain. The intrinsic worth of the wood from each part of the tree differs - that from the root being the most expensive and the branches having the lowest price.

A cheaper product is liable to warp, or in case it is taken to warmer climes, will crack or shrink. Knots are usually concealed skillfully in the sawing, as it is difficult, though not impossible, to mask them while carving. Carving is the demonstration of the carver's skill, and walnut is eminently suitable for this, being one of the strongest varieties of wood.

There are several varieties of carving-deep carving usually with dragon or lotus flower motifs, two inches deep or more; shallow carving, half an inch deep done all over the flat surface; open or lattice work, usually depicting the Chinar motif; and most popularly, semi carving, which is a thin panel along the rim of a surface, with perhaps a Centre motif. The advantage of the semi-carving is that it allows the grain of wood to be displayed, together with the carver's skill. Naturally deep carving with all the skill and labour required is the most expensive.

Copper and Silverware: Shops in local market of the old city abound with objects of copper lining the walls, the floor and even the ceiling. One can see craftsmen engraving objects of household utility like samovars, bowls, plates and trays. There are floral, stylized, geometric, leaf and even calligraphic motifs that are engraved or embossed on copper, and occasionally silver, to cover the entire surface with intricate designs which are then oxidized, the better to stand out from the background. The work known as 'naqash' determines the price of the object, as does the weight.

MONUMENTS

Jammu & Kashmir has a good share of Indian historical and archaeological legacy. There has been a very unique and glorious tradition of the people of the State of preaching and worshipping of each other's religions and pilgrimage centres. There are well-renowned Hindu shrines co-existing with the equally famous Muslim pilgrimage centres that are held in highest esteem by the people of every faith.

Buddhism, which is still followed in the Laddakh region of the State, has its origin in the valley and was preached and disseminated by the Kashmiri scholars in its earlier days. There are some wonderful examples of this communal harmony in pilgrimage centres like the one at Hari Parbat where monuments of all three religions - a temple, mosque and gurudwara are standing side by side. Some of the important shrines and monuments of the region have been covered below:

Hazratbal Mosque: Situated in a village on the western shores of the Dal Lake opposite Nishat Bagh, it is a pristine white marble edifice casting its reflection in the waters of the lake. It is revered for the fact that it houses a hair of the prophet Muhammad, which is displayed to the public on religious occasions. Fairs are held on such occasions. People throng to the place every Friday to offer their prayers. Unlike the other mosques in Srinagar, which have a pagoda like roof, Hazratbal is the only mosque to have a domed roof. Mosque in Srinagar; the others having distinct pagoda like roofs.

Jami Masjid: Situated in the heart of the old city of Srinagar, this huge mosque is visited by thousands of people who congregate here for the Friday prayers. The largest mosque in Kashmir, it is built around a courtyard with 370 wooden pillars to support it. Originally built by Sultan Sikandar in 1400, and enlarged by his son, Zain-ul- Abidin, it is a typical example of Indo-Saracenic architecture. Destroyed thrice by fire in 1479, 1620 and 1674 respectively and rebuilt each time, the mosque of today was repaired during the reign of Maharaja Pratap Singh. The principal features of the mosque are the four minars and eight wooden columns as support.

Shankaracharya Temple: Believed to have been built at the auspicious site of Takht-e-Sulaiman, the sacred temple of Shankaracharya occupies the top of the hills in the southeast of Srinagar. Dating back to 250 BC, it is believed that it was the place where the great philosopher and saint Shankaracharya stayed when he visited Kashmir ten centuries ago to revive Sanatan Dharma. It was then that this place came to be known by his name instead of its former name Gopadri, an earlier edifice built on the same site by king Lalitaditya in the 6th century AD. Built on a high octagonal plinth and approached by a flight of steps, it has sidewalls that once bore inscriptions and the main surviving shrine consists of a circular cell. A modern ceiling covers the inner sanctum and an inscription in Persian traces its origin to the reign of Emperor Shah Jehan. The original ceiling was dome- shaped and the brick roof is not more than a century old.

Khanqah of Shah Hamadan: Situated on the banks of the River Jhelum, it is the first mosque ever built in Srinagar. The Shah Hamadan whose full name was Mir Sayed Ali Hamadni built the original mosque in 1395. Shah-i-Hamdan came from Persia in the 13th century and was responsible for the spread of Islam in Kashmir. Khanqah-i-Mualla was the place where he used to offer prayers. The Khanqah is a wooden structure whose chief aesthetic feature is its beautifully carved eaves and hanging bells. The interiors are richly carved and painted, and the antique chandeliers give it an air of magnificence.

Hari Parbat Fort & Temple of Sharika Devi: Built in the 18th century, atop the Sharika Hill, Atta Mohammed Khan constructed the fort from 1776 though the surrounding wall was built by Akbar in the 16th century and is much older. It has two gates, the Kathi and Sangin Darwaza. The Kathi is the main entrance with Persian commemorative inscriptions surrounding it while the Sangin is more ornate with sculptured windows on either side. Mow used as an arsenal, the fort contains a temple revered for its image of the Goddess Sharika, a form of Durga.

Makhdoom Sahib: The shrine, situated to the south of Hari Parbat, is dedicated to Makhdoom Sahib or Hazrat Sultan and is revered by Muslims and Hindus alike.

Chhatti Padshahi Gurudwara: Situated just outside the southern gate of Hari Parbat fort, Chatti Padshahi is one of the most important Sikh Gurudwaras in Kashmir. It is dedicated to the sixth guru of Sikhism who stopped here to preach occasionally while he was travelling through Kashmir.

Martand: The most memorable and beautiful work of Emperor Lalitaditya of Surya (meaning 'solar') dynasty is the construction of spacious Martand temple dedicated to the Sun god, Bhaskar. The style of the construction of the temple and the skill of the makers are rare in the history of the world. Now, in ruins, it is still appreciable for its design, beauty and art. Martand temple is a mirror of the art and skill of Kashmiri Hindus. In its backdrop are the snowcapped mountains and it is built with strong and square limestone. Its pillars have a Greek pattern that lends gorgeousness to this edifice.

Kheer Bhawani: Situated at Tullamulla in the Srinagar district, this spring is the most sacred place for Hindus in Kashmir. Hindus must abstain from meat on the days when they visit Kheer Bhavani or the milk goddess and offer her sugar, milk, rice and flowers. An annual festival is held here in May or June when a number of devotees visit the place to offer prayers and seek the blessings of the deity. The beautiful spring of clear water overshadowed by splendid shady trees and full of sacred fish adds an ethereal beauty to the place.

Awantipur: 29 km. from Srinagar, the famous Awantipur temples are believed to have been built in honour of God Mahadev by Awanti Varman. The temples, although in ruins, are of great archaeological interest. King Avantivarman founded the city in the 9th century. There are two main temples, one of which is Shiva-Avantishvara, which is larger and marked by massive walls some half a mile beneath the town on the outskirts of village Jaubror. Reduced to ruins now, the place almost lost its previous grandeur, and has been reduced to ruins, though it is still visited by the devout. The sculptured reliefs principally found on the walls of the entrance and the flank walls of the stairs depict men and women in the acts of drinking, lovemaking and other such merriments. The base is either a plain square block with the upper edge rounded off or is elaborately molded. Half a mile up is Avantisvami-Vishnu, a better-preserved temple.

SPORTS IN JAMMU AND KASHMIR

Popular sports in Jammu and Kashmir include cricket and football along with sports like golf, winter sports, water sports and adventure sports. Jammu and Kashmir has produced international and national level players including Gul Dev (first Kashmiri Olympian), Aamir Aziz, Chain Singh, Iqra Rasool, Mehrajuddin Wadoo, Mithun Manhas, Abid Nabi, Parvez Rasool, Tajamal Islam and Palak Kaur.

Snowmobile riders enjoying themselves at the 5th National Winter Games at Gulmarg, Kashmir on February 22, 2008.

Against the background of the Kashmir conflict and tension in the state, government initiatives in the sports sector are promoted specifically trying to draw the youth away from the conflict.

The Indian Army also conducts sporting activities for the youth in the region through various welfare initiative such as Operation Sadbhavana. Lack of infrastructure, politicization, lack of support are other issues hampering growth of the sports in the region.

Shera, the mascot of the Commonwealth Games Delhi 2010 takes a ride on Dal Lake

The sports fraternity of Srinagar taking the Queen's Baton for the Delhi 2010 Commonwealth Gamesfor a ride in Srinagar

Sporting activities

Cricket in Jammu and Kashmir

Cricket is one of the most popular sports in Jammu and Kashmir. Recently Ifran Pathan was made the mentor and coach of the Jammu and Kashmir cricket team. The team participates in the events such as the Ranjhi Trophy and Vijay Hazare Trophy. Popular players to have come from the region include Parvez Rasool, Mithun Manhas and Manzoor Dar who have played T20 IPL matches for team such as Sunrisers Hyderabad and Kings XI Punjab. Other cricketers from Jammu and Kashmir include Jasia Akhtar who was the first women from Jammu and Kashmir to be selected for the India women's national cricket team and Amir Hussain Lone who is the captain of Jammu and Kashmir's para cricket team.

There is criticism related to excessive politicization and lack of professionalism and support in development of the sport in the region.

Kashmiri youth playing cricket at top of Wular Lake, Bandipora district, Jammu and Kashmir.

Football in Jammu and Kashmir

Football first came to Jammu and Kashmir in 1891-92 by

Tyndale Biscoe. The first time a football team from the region participated in the Santosh Trophy was in 1964.

Teams from Jammu and Kashmir which play in the I-League are Real Kashmir F.C. (division one) and Lonestar Kashmir F.C. (division two). Mehrajuddin Wadoo from Srinagar has represented the Indian National Football Team and also plays in the Indian Super League.

Jammu and Kashmir has produced nineteen international players (from the school level to the senior team) such as Abdul Majeed Kakroo.

Players from the region have been part of top football teams in India such as Mohun Bagan A.C. and East Bengal F.C. (such as Ishfaq Ahmed).

Basit Ahmed and Mohammed Renbar were chosen to play football with Sociedad Deportiva Lenense Proinastur (SD Lenense), a third division Spanish team, part of a public outreach program of Central Reserve Police Force (CRPF) and J&K Football Association.

Other initiatives such as a football team for every village in the Kashmir Valley has also been initiated by the government in 2017.

Marathons in Jammu and Kashmir

Marathons that have been conducted in the region include the Ladakh Marathon, the Great Tibetan Marathon and the Kashmir International Half Marathon. The Ladakh Marathon is recognised by Association of International Marathons and Distance Races and is one of the highest marathon in the world.

Adventure Sports

Jammu and Kashmir, with its hilly terrain and swift flowing rivers, offers great scope for adventure sports such as Heliskiing, Ice Skating, Ice Hockey, water skiing, paragliding and mountaineering and Snowboarding.

Tsewang Paljor and Tsewang Samanla from Leh was part India's first team to reach the summit of Mount Everest (from the North Col side). Sonam Wangyal, also from Leh, climbed Mount Everest when he was 23, making him the youngest person to do so at the time.

Infrastructure and institutions

Jammu and Kashmir has 19 stadiums, 23 training centers, three indoor sports complexes and 43 government maintained playing fields. This includes Sher-i-Kashmir Stadium, TRC turf ground, Bakshi Stadium, Amar Singh Club Ground, Gandhi Memorial Science College Ground and the Maulana Azad Stadium.

Srinagar District also has two golf courses - Kashmir Golf Club and Royal Spring Golf Course.

Institutions such as the Jawahar Institute of Mountaineering and Winter Sports provides mountaineering, skiing and adventure courses.

Hamid Ansari, the former Vice President of India visits the Jawahar Institute of Mountaineering and Winter Sports, at Pahalgam, Jammu & Kashmir on September 15, 2012

Royal Springs Golf Course, Srinagar

Synthetic Turf Football Stadium, TRC Polo Ground

The TRC ground is Jammu and Kashmir's first football stadium. It has imported synthetic football turf. The synthetic turf for the stadium has been imported from Italy. The stadium has a capacity for 15000 spectators. The field is of international standard size.

Sher-i-Kashmir Stadium

Sher-i-Kashmir Stadium is a cricket stadium located in Srinagar. It is home to the JKCA and Jammu and Kashmir cricket team which represents the Indian state of Jammu and Kashmir in the Ranji Trophyand other domestic tournaments in the country. National Cricket Academy is currently constructing an indoor complex at the stadium.

Jammu & Kashmir State Sports Council

The Jammu & Kashmir State Sports Council objectives include promoting sports activities in the State among the student and non-student youth, creating and developing sports infrastructure in various parts of the State and providing financial assistance and grants. The Organisation is headed by the Chief Minister of Jammu and Kashmir and the Sports Minister as its President and Vice-President respectively. The Sports Council functions at State, Divisional and District level.

Awards

The government of Jammu & Kashmir has introduced various awards to inspire not only the sports people, but also coaches and sports associations. Following are some of these awards:

- Sher-I-Kashmir Award and Medal
- Maharaja Ranjit Singh Award and Medal
- Parshuran Awards and Medals
- Brig Rajinder Singh Award and Medal for Men
- Madri-I-Meharban Award and Medal
- Chief Minister's Gold Rolling Trophy

Sports Associations

There are over 40 official registered sports associations in the region such the J&K Cricket Association and the J&K Football Association. Other associations under the sports council include the J&K Yoga Association, J&K Cycling Association and the J&K Billiard and Snooker Association. Associations have also been set up for the deaf as well for veterans.

3

Government and Politics

INTRODUCTION

Jammu and Kashmir is the only state in India which enjoys special autonomy under Article 370 of the Constitution of India, according to which no law enacted by the Parliament of India, except for those in the field of defence, communication and foreign policy, will be extendable in Jammu and Kashmir unless it is ratified by the state legislature of Jammu and Kashmir. Subsequently, jurisdiction of the Supreme Court of India over Jammu and Kashmir has been extended.

Jammu and Kashmir is the only Indian state to have its own official state flag along with national flag and constitution. Indians from other states cannot purchase land or property in the state. Designed by the then ruling National Conference, the flag of Jammu and Kashmir features a ploughon a red background symbolising labour; it replaced the Maharaja's state flag. The three stripes represent the three distinct administrative divisions of the state, namely Jammu, Valley of Kashmir, and Ladakh.

In 1990, an Armed Forces Act, which gives special powers to the Indian security forces, has been enforced in Jammu and Kashmir. The decision to invoke this act was criticised by the

Human Rights Watch. Amnesty International has strongly condemned the implementation of this Act that grants virtual immunity to security forces from prosecution. Minar Pimple, Senior Director of Global Operations at Amnesty International states.

Like all the states of India, Jammu and Kashmir has a multi-party democratic system of governance with a bicameral legislature. At the time of drafting the Constitution of Jammu and Kashmir, 100 seats were earmarked for direct elections from territorial constituencies. Of these, 25 seats were reserved for the areas of Jammu and Kashmir State that came under Pakistani occupation; this was reduced to 24 after the 12th amendment of the Constitution of Jammu and Kashmir:

"The territory of the State shall comprise all the territories which on the fifteenth day of August 1947, were under the sovereignty or suzerainty of the Ruler of the State" and Section 48 therein states that, "Notwithstanding anything contained in section 47, until the area of the State under the occupations of Pakistan ceases to so occupied and the people residing in that area elect their representatives (a) twenty-five seats in the Legislative Assembly shall remain vacant and shall not be taken into account for reckoning the total member-ship of the Assembly; and the said area shall be excluded in delimiting the territorial Constituencies Under Section 47".

After a delimitation in 1988, the total number of seats increased to 111, of which 87 were within Indian-administered territory. The Jammu & Kashmir Assembly is the only state in India to have a 6-year term, in contrast to the norm of a 5-year term followed in every other state's Assembly. There was indication from the previous INC Government to bring parity with the other states, but this does not seem to have received the required support to pass into law.

Influential political parties include the Jammu & Kashmir National Conference (NC), the Indian National Congress (INC), the Jammu and Kashmir People's Democratic Party (PDP), the Bharatiya Janata Party (BJP) and other smaller regional parties.

After dominating Kashmir's politics for years, the National Conference's influence waned in 2002, when INC and PDP formed a political alliance and rose to power. Under the power-sharing agreement, INC leader Ghulam Nabi Azad replaced PDP's Mufti Mohammad Sayeed as the Chief Minister of Jammu and Kashmir in late 2005. However, in 2008, PDP withdrew its support from the government on the issue of temporary diversion of nearly 40 acres (16 ha) of land to the Sri Amarnath Shrine Board. In the 2008 Kashmir Elections that were held from 17 November to 24 December, the National Conference party and the Congress party together won enough seats in the state assembly to form a ruling alliance. In the 2014 election, the voter turnout was recorded at 65% – the highest in the history of the state. The results gave a fractured mandate to either parties – the PDP won 28 seats, BJP 25, NC 15 and INC 12. After 2 months of deliberations and president's rule, the BJP and the PDP announced an agreement for a coalition government, and PDP patron Mufti Mohammad Sayeed was sworn-in as CM for a second term, with Nirmal Singh of the BJP sworn-in as deputy CM. This also marked the first time in 35 years that the BJP was a coalition partner in the state government.

The state has two autonomous councils in Ladakh, these are the LAHDC Leh and LAHDC Kargil.

Separatist insurgency and militancy since 1989

In 1989, a widespread popular and armed insurgency started in Kashmir. After the 1987 state legislative assembly election, some of the results were disputed. This resulted in the formation of militant wings and marked the beginning of the Mujahadeen insurgency, which continues to this day. India contends that the insurgency was largely started by Afghan mujahadeen who entered the Kashmir valley following the end of the Soviet–Afghan War. Yasin Malik, a leader of one faction of the Jammu Kashmir Liberation Front, was one of the Kashmiris to organise militancy in Kashmir, along with Ashfaq Majid Wani and Farooq Ahmed Dar (alias Bitta Karate). Since 1995, Malik has renounced the use of violence and calls for strictly peaceful methods to resolve the dispute. Malik developed differences with one of the senior leaders, Farooq Siddiqui (alias Farooq Papa), for shunning demands for an independent Kashmir and trying to cut a deal with the Indian Prime Minister. This resulted in a split in which Bitta Karate, Salim Nanhaji, and other senior comrades joined Farooq Papa. Pakistan claims these insurgents are Jammu and Kashmir citizens and are rising up against the Indian army as part of an independence movement. Amnesty International has accused security forces in Indian-controlled Kashmir of exploiting an Armed Forces (Special Powers) Act that enables them to "hold prisoners without trial". The group argues that the law, which allows security forces to detain individuals for up to two years without presenting charges violates prisoners' human rights. In 2011, the state humans right commission said it had evidence that 2,156 bodies had been buried in 40 graves over the last 20 years. The authorities deny such accusations. The security forces say the unidentified dead are militants who may have originally come from outside India. They also say that many of the missing people have crossed into Pakistan-administered Kashmir to engage in militancy. However, according to the state human rights commission, among the identified bodies 574 were those of "disappeared locals", and according to Amnesty International's annual human rights report (2012) it was sufficient for "belying the security forces' claim that they were militants".

Separatist violence in the region has been observed to decline. However, following the unrest in 2008, which included more than 500,000 protesters at a rally on 18 August, secessionist movements gained a boost. Further the 2016–17 Kashmir Unrest culminated in the deaths of more than 90 civilians, with over 15,000 civilians injured.

The 2009 edition of the Freedom in the World (report) by the US-based NGO Freedom House rated Jammu and Kashmir as "Partly Free", while in comparison, the same report rated Pakistan-administered Kashmir as "Not Free." However, in the same report the Political rights and Civil liberties scored 6 and

5 respectively for Azad Kashmir while as for Jammu and Kashmir the scores were 5 and 4 respectively.

Six policemen, including a sub-inspector were killed in an ambush by militants in Anantnag, Jammu and Kashmir on June 15, 2017, by trespassing militants of the Pakistan-based Lashkar-e-Taiba. 116 illegal trespassing cases along the India-Pak border in Jammu and Kashmir were reported in 2015 and 2016, including 88 in 2016. A total of 59 Army personnel have lost their lives in counter-terror operations in J&K since 2016.

POLITICS OF JAMMU AND KASHMIR

The state of Jammu and Kashmir has historically consisted of four political regions. Ladakh towards the east bordering China, Jammutowards the south bordering the states of Himachal Pradesh, Punjab and Pakistan, Kashmir Valley towards the west bordering Pakistan administered Kashmir and Baltistan areas towards the North bordering Xinjiang and Gilgit Baltistan. Baltistan and a part of Kashmir are under Pakistan control. Aksai Chin, claimed by India to be a part of Ladakh, is under Chinese control, while the rest is under Indian control. Pakistan and Indian controlled parts are separated by Line of Control (LOC).

Like all the states of India, Indian administered parts of Jammu & Kashmir have a multi-party democratic system of governance. Main political parties include the Jammu & Kashmir National Conference (NC), the Indian National Congress (Congress), Bharatiya Janata Party (BJP)and the Jammu and Kashmir Peoples Democratic Party (PDP). Presently, PDP with 28 seats is the 1st largest and Bharatiya Janata Partywith 25 seats is the second largest party in 2014 election in the 87-member house.

The Constitution of India grants Jammu and Kashmir special autonomous status as a temporary provision through Article 370. However, some Muslim Kashmiris demand greater autonomy and sovereignty and some even demand independence from India, while some non-Muslims would like to see the state fully integrated into India. A part of Kashmiri Muslims also have inclination towards Pakistan since a small part of Kashmir is under Pakistan Control. There has also been a number of separatist movements, both political and militant, mostly led by hardline Muslim leaders. However, in recent years Kashmiri Muslims have been leaning towards being in India due to economic reasons.

Jammu and Kashmir is the only Indian state that has its own flag. Designed by the Government of India, the state flag of Jammu and Kashmir is the native plough on a red background which is a symbol of labour. The three stripes represent the three administrative divisions of the state, namely Jammu, Valley of Kashmir, and Ladakh.

Furthermore, a 2008 report by United Nations High Commissioner for Refugees determined that State of Jammu and Kashmir is one and only 'Partly free' state in India.

GOVERNMENT OF JAMMU AND KASHMIR

The Government of Jammu and Kashmir is the supreme governing authority of the Indian state of Jammu and Kashmir and its 3 Divisions and 22 districts. It consists of an executive, led by the Governor of Jammu and Kashmir, a judiciary and a legislative branch.

Like other states in India, the head of state of Jammu and Kashmir is the Governor, appointed by the President of India on the advice of the Central government. His or her post is largely ceremonial. The Chief Minister, is the head of government. Srinagar and Jammuare the summer and winter capitals of Jammu and Kashmir.

The present Legislature of Jammu and Kashmir is bicameral, consisting of a lower house (Vidhan Sabha) of 89 Member of the Legislative Assembly (M.L.A) and an upper house (Vidhan Parishad) of 36 members. Its term is 6 years, unless sooner dissolved. The assembly is housed in the "Old Secretariat" in Srinagar, the former Sher Garhi Palace. The Jammu and Kashmir High Court has branches in Srinagar and Jammu.

CONSTITUTION OF JAMMU AND KASHMIR

The Constitution of Jammu and Kashmir is the legal document which establishes the framework of government at state level in Indian state of Jammu and Kashmir. The present constitution was adopted on 17 November 1956, and came into effect on 26 January 1957. As of 2002, 29 amendments have been affected to the Constitution.

The Constitution of India grants special status to Jammu and Kashmir among Indian states, and it is the only state in India to have a separate constitution. Article 370 of the Constitution of India states that Parliament of India and the Union Government jurisdiction extends over limited matters with respect to State of Jammu and Kashmir, and in all other matters not specifically vested in Federal governments, actions have to be supported by state legislature. Also, unlike other states, residual powers are vested in state government. Because of these constitutional provisions, the State of Jammu and Kashmir enjoys autonomy not enjoyed by other states. Among notable and visible differences with other states, till 1965, the head of state in Jammu and Kashmir was styled Sadr-e-Riyasat, whereas in other state, the title was Governor, and head of government was styled Prime Minister in place of Chief Minister in other states.

Historical aspect

India gained its independence from the United Kingdom on midnight of 15 August 1947 IST, and simultaneously Pakistan was created as a new country as a result of the partition of India. Jammu and Kashmir, then a princely state under suzerainty of British Monarch, and ruled by the Maharaja Hari Singh tried to avoid declaring his state's accession to either of the two dominions at the time of independence (although that was not an option under the Indian Independence Act, 1947). A Muslim majority state ruled by Hindu Maharaja Hari Singh (then the ruler of the state), government of the state signed a standstill agreement with Pakistan. However, on 6 October 1947, Pakistani Muslim tribes, supported by the government of Pakistan, attacked Jammu and Kashmir on the behest of Pakistan to achieve forcible accession to Pakistan. Maharaja Hari Singh requested assistance from India, and when India requested an Instrument of Accession to India, Maharaja signed it so that India could help in defense.

The Instrument of Accession (IoA) gave only limited powers to the Government of India, only about the three subject matters of Foreign affairs, Defence and Communications. It was similar to several hundred others IoA signed between the Government of India and other princely states. Whereas the other states later signed merger agreements, the relationship of Jammu and Kashmir with the Union of India was governed by special circumstances. In view of them, the Article 370 was incorporated in the Constitution. The Constitution of Jammu and Kashmir, which Maharaja (later Sadr-e-Riyasat) Dr. Karan Singh signed into law in 1957, is still in force.

Salient Features

The Constitution, as of 2002, has 158 articles divided into 13 parts and 7 schedules. The divisions of articles is as follows. The numbers in braces after show the articles included in a particular part.

Part I: Preliminary (1-2)

Part II: The State (3-5)

Part III: Permanent Residents (6-10)

Part IV: Directive Principles of State Policy (11-25)

Part V: The Executive (26-45)

- The Governor (26-34)
- The Council of Ministers (35-41)
- The Advocate General (42)
- Conduct of Government Business (43-45)

Part VI: The State Legislature (46-92)

- Composition of the State Legislature (46-50)
- General Provisions (51-56)
- Officers of the State Legislature (57-63)

- Conduct of Business (64-67)
- Disqualification of Members (68-71)
- Powers, Privileges and Immunities of the State Legislature and Its members (72-73)
- Legislative Procedure (74-78)
- Procedure In Financial Matters (79-84)
- Procedure Generally (85-90)
- Legislative power of the Governor (91)
- Breakdown of Constitutional Machinery (92)

Part VII The High Court (93-113)

- Subordinate Courts (109-113)

Part VIII: Finance, Property and Contracts (114-123)

Part IX: The Public Services (124-137)

- The Public Service Commission (128-137)

Part X: Elections (138-142)

Part XI: Miscellaneous Provisions (143-146)

Part XII: Amendment of the Constitution (147)

Part XIII: Transmonal Issues (153-158)

Articles 148 to 152 have been omitted in Part XIII.

Schedules:

- *Schedule I: Omitted* (Repealed)
- Schedule II: Emoluments, Allowances and Privileges of the Governor
- Schedule III: Salaries and allowances of the Speaker and Deputy Speaker of the Legislative Assembly and the Chairman and the Deputy Chairman of the Legislative Council
- Schedule IV: Salaries, allowances and other conditions of service of the Judges of the High Court.
- Schedule V: Forms of Oaths or affirmations
- Schedule VI: Regional Languages
- Schedule VII: Provision as to disqualification on ground of defections

Although India has a unitary citizenship, Constitution of Jammu & Kashmir defines a concept of Permanent Residency, in Part III. This concept is functionally similar to citizenship, and permanent residents of the State enjoy rights not enjoyed by non-residents. Citizens of India who do not have permanent residency in the State have limited property ownership rights.

Preamble

Preamble to the Constitution of Jammu and Kashmir is as quoted below.

"WE, THE PEOPLE OF THE STATE OF JAMMU AND KASHMIR,

having solemnly resolved, in pursuance of the accession of this State to India which took place on the twenty sixth day of October, 1947, to further define the existing relationship of the State with the Union of India as an integral part thereof, and to secure to ourselves-

JUSTICE, social, economic and political;

LIBERTY of thought, expression, belief, faith and worship;

EQUALITY of status and of opportunity; and to promote among us all;

FRATERNITY assuring the dignity of the individual and the unity of the nation;

IN OUR CONSTITUENT ASSEMBLY this seventeenth day of November, 1956, do HEREBY ADOPT, ENACT AND GIVE

TO OURSELVES THIS CONSTITUTION."

—-*Preamble of Constitution of Jammu & Kashmir.*

The preamble resembles almost verbatim to the Preamble to the Constitution of India.

Jurisdiction of Parliament

Under Part XXI of the Constitution of India, which deals with "Temporary, Transitional and Special provisions", the State of

Jammu and Kashmir has been accorded special status under Article 370. Even though included in 1st Schedule as 15th state, all the provisions of the Constitution which are applicable to other states are not applicable to Jammu and Kashmir. Government of India can declare emergency in Jammu and Kashmir and impose Governor's rule in certain conditions. Matters related to Defense, Foreign relations, Communication and Finance of Jammu and Kashmir is under jurisdiction of Constitution of India.

Union Legislature has very limited jurisdiction in case of Jammu and Kashmir in comparison with other states. Till 1963, Parliament could legislate on subjects contained in the Union List, and had no jurisdiction in case of Concurrent List under 7th Schedule with Jammu and Kashmir. The Parliament has no power to legislate Preventive Detention laws for the state; only the state legislature has the power to do so.

Emergency Provisions

The Union of India has no power to declare Financial Emergency under Article 370 in the state. The Union can declare emergency in the state only in case of War or External Aggression. No proclamation of emergency made on the grounds of internal disturbance or imminent danger thereof shall have effect in relation to the state unless (a) it is made at the request or with the concurrence of the government of the state; or (b) where it has not been so made, it is applied subsequently by the President to that state at the request or with the concurrence of the government of that state. In December 1964, Articles 356 and 357 were extended to the state.

Fundamental Duties, Directive Principles and Fundamental Rights

Part IV (Directive Principles of the State Policy) and Part IVA (Fundamental Duties) of the Constitution are not applicable to Jammu and Kashmir. In addition to other fundamental rights, Articles 19(1)(f) and 31(2) of the Constitution are still applicable to Jammu and Kashmir; hence the Fundamental Right to property is still guaranteed in this state.It is the only state which does not have to give a detailed record on the money flowing in the state and where it is used and how. In the Indian Constitutional history only one Fundamental Right has been added so far and that is Right to Education. This right too has not been extended to Jammu and Kashmir.

Official Languages

Provisions of Part XVII of the Constitution apply to Jammu and Kashmir only insofar as they relate to (i) the official language of the Union; (ii) the official language for communication between one state and another; or between a state and the Union; and (iii) language of the proceedings in the Supreme Court. Urdu is the official language of the state but use of English is permitted for official purposes unless the state legislature provides otherwise.

Relations with Government of India

- Article 3 in part 2 of the Jammu and Kashmir constitution reads as, "*Relationship of the State with the Union of India*:-The State of Jammu and Kashmir is and shall be an integral part of the Union of India."
- Article 5 of the part 2 is about extent of "Executive" and "Legislative" powers of the state which tells that Jammu and Kashmir Legislative Assembly has executive and legislative power of all matters except those with respect to which Parliament of India has power to make laws for the State under the provisions of the Constitution of India. Sectors in which Government of India can make laws for Jammu and Kashmir includes Defense sector, Foreign affairs, Finance and Communication.
- Article 147 of Part 12 is about amendment of the Jammu and Kashmir Constitution which states that, "No Bill shall be introduced or moved in State Legislative Assembly to amend or change above mentioned articles 3 and 5."

Relations with Pakistan administered Kashmir

- Article 48 of Part VI of Jammu and Kashmir constitution defines Pakistan Administered Kashmir as "Pakistan Occupied Territory".
- There are currently 87 seats in Jammu and Kashmir State assembly, but article 48 of Jammu and Kashmir constitution also recognizes 24 seats from Pakistan administered Kashmir and mentions that these 24 seats will remain vacant till Pakistan ceases the "occupation" of Kashmir and the said area shall be excluded in delimiting the territorial constituencies till that time.

Miscellaneous

Certain special rights have been granted to the permanent residents of Jammu and Kashmir with regard to employment under the state, acquisition of immovable property in the state, settlement in the state, and scholarship and other forms of aid as the state government may provide.

The 5th Schedule pertaining to the administration and control of Schedule Areas and Scheduled Tribes and the 6th Schedule pertaining to administration of tribal areas are not applicable to the state of Jammu and Kashmir. The Provisions of the State Constitution (except those relating to the relationship of the state with the Union) may be amended by an Act of the Legislative Assembly of the state passed by not less than two-thirds of its membership. If such amendment seeks to affect Governor or Election Commission, it needs President's assent to come into effect. No amendment of the Constitution of India shall extend to Jammu and Kashmir unless so extended by an order of Jammu and Kashmir President under Article 370(1).

No Bill or amendment can be introduced or moved in either House of the Legislature which seeks to make any change in the provisions that (a) the State of Jammu and Kashmir is and shall be an integral part of the Union of India (Art. 3) (b) the executive and legislative power of the State does not extend to matters those with respect to which Parliament has power to make laws for the State under the provisions of the Constitution of India (Art. 5), (c) of the Constitution of India as applicable in relation to the State (Art.147 (c) and Art. 147. (Art. 147(a)).

ELECTIONS IN JAMMU AND KASHMIR

Elections in Jammu and Kashmir are conducted to elect members of the Jammu and Kashmir Legislative Assembly and the Lok Sabha(House of People). There are 87 assembly constituencies and 6 Lok sabha constituencies (parliamentary constituencies). Elections in the state also include Panchayat elections which are held for sarpanch and panch constituencies as part of the Panchayati Raj system.Municipal elections have been held in the state only four times since 1947, with the October 2018 elections being the fifth time they will be held.

A voter coming out after casting his vote from a polling booth of Budgamduring the 4th Phase of General Election 2009 on 7 May 2009. (The raised finger indicates the indelible inkfrom voting)

Jammu and Kashmir National Conference (JKNC), Jammu & Kashmir People's Democratic Party (PDP) and Indian National Congress (INC)have been the dominant political parties in Jammu and Kashmir, but in recent years the vote share of

Bharatiya Janata Party has increased considerably, from 12.45% in 2008 to 23% in 2014.

Main Political Parties

This list includes state parties as well as national parties. It also include political parties which no longer exist

- MC: All Jammu and Kashmir Muslim Conference, founded in 1932, renamed JKNC in 1939
- JKNC: Jammu & Kashmir National Conference, merged with INC in 1965
- PC: Jammu & Kashmir Political Conference, separated from JKNC in 1947
- PF: Jammu & Kashmir Plebiscite Front, founded in 1955, renamed as JKNC in 1977
- ANC: Awami National Conference, break-away faction of JKNC, 1984-1986
- INC: Indian National Congress
- PDP: Jammu & Kashmir People's Democratic Party, split from INC in 1987
- PP: Jammu & Kashmir Praja Parishad, merged with BJS in 1963
- BJS: Bharatiya Jana Sangh, merged into Janata Party in 1977, revived as BJP in 1980
- Janata: Janata Party, formed in 1977, disintegrated in 1980
- BJP: Bharatiya Janata Party
- Jamaat: Jamaat-e-Islami Kashmir, formed soon after 1947, contested elections since 1972 (under the MUF umbrella in 1987)
- MUF: Muslim United Front, a coalition of Muslim nationalist groups (Jamaat-e-Islami, Ummat-e-Islami, Anjunmane Ittehad-ul-Musalmeen) that contested elections in 1987.

- PSP: Praja Socialist Party, 1953-1977, merging into the Janata Party in 1977
- JD: Janata Dal
- HM: Harijan Mandal, 1951-1972
- Panthers: Jammu and Kashmir National Panthers Party, formed in 1982

Lok Sabha elections

Jammu and Kashmir has taken part in 12 general elections to the Lok Sabha of India. The first time that Jammu & Kashmir sent elected members to the Lok Sabha was in 1967. Elections were not held in 1990 in Jammu and Kashmir due to insurgency in the region.

JAMMU AND KASHMIR LEGISLATIVE ASSEMBLY ELECTION, 2014

The Jammu and Kashmir Legislative Assembly election, 2014 was held in the Indian state of Jammu and Kashmir in five phases from 25 November – 20 December 2014. Voters elected 87 members to the Jammu and Kashmir Legislative Assembly, which ends its six-year term on 19 January 2015. The results were declared on 23 December 2014. Voter-verified paper audit trail (VVPAT) along with EVMs were used in 3 assembly seats out of 87 in Jammu Kashmir elections.

Background and campaign

Before the election, Indian National Congress broke its alliance with Jammu and Kashmir National Conferenceand contested on all seats in the assembly.

Campaigning before the elections was aggressive and robust. Following the huge victory of Bharatiya Janata Party in the Indian parliamentary election, the BJP turned its attention towards J&K and campaigned on the promise of 'development'. This included a visit from the Prime Minister of India, Narendra Modi in support of the local BJP campaign.

Boycott Calls

- Hardline separatist All Parties Hurriyat Conference leader Syed Ali Shah Geelani had appealed to people of Kashmir to boycott the 2014 Jammu and Kashmir Legislative Assembly elections completely, arguing that "India has been holding elections in the Valley using the power of gun and so such an exercise is not legitimate." He added, "My appeal to the youth in particular is that the sacrifices rendered by the people must be safeguarded and, hence, in no way should vote during elections."
- Separatists were propagating the poll boycott campaign through video clips on social networking sites and applications, including Facebook and WhatsApp.
- A four-minute video clip has gone viral on social sites with messages of chairmen of both hardline and moderate factions of Hurriyat Conference and Dukhtaran-e-Millat chief Asiya Andrabi. The video message sent through WhatsApp and shared on Facebook and Twitter asked the people to boycott the coming polls.
- Video also showed Hurriyat hawk Syed Ali Shah Geelani addressing a gathering via phone urging youth not to undermine the mission of 'martyrs'. Moderate Hurriyat chairman Mirwaiz Umar Farooq is seen posing for the camera with the appeal that polls must be boycotted 'en masse'.

Voting

The polls were carried out in five phases. Despite several boycott calls by hurriyat leaders, elections recorded highest voters turnout in last 25 years. Voters turnout was more than 65% which is higher than usual voting percentage in other states of India.

The European Parliament, on the behalf of European Union, welcomed the smooth conduct of the State Legislative Elections in the Jammu and Kashmir. The EU in its message said that,

"The high voter turnout figure proves that democracy is firmly rooted in India. The EU would like to congratulate India and its democratic system for conduct of fair elections, unmarred by violence, in the state of Jammu and Kashmir".

Date	Seats	Turnout
Tuesday 25 November	15	71.28%
Tuesday 2 December	18	71%
Tuesday 9 December	16	58.89%
Sunday 14 December	18	49%
Saturday 20 December	20	76%
Total	87	65.23%

The European Parliament also takes cognizance of the fact that a large number of Kashmiri voters turned out despite calls for the boycott of elections by certain separatist forces. However, elected Jammu and Kashmir Chief Minister Mufti Muhammad Sayeed said, "If God forbid the Hurriyat and the militants tried to disrupt the elections these would not have been as participative as they had been. They (Pakistan) also allowed these elections to take place." Ruling Party president Mehbooba Mufti also defended Mufti's remarks. While taking dig at Mufti's statement former Chief minister of Jammu and Kashmir and leader of opposition in Rajya Sabha Ghulam Nabi Azad said that, "In fact, Pakistan and militant groups tried their best to destabilise the democratic process in the state."

Government formation

Three days after the results, the JKN approached the BJP for a meeting to try and form a government. As part of the deal, Nirmal Kumar Singh was to be the chief minister and JKN's MLA Ali Mohammad Sagar was to be his deputy. The deal fell through after a revolt in the JKN. The BJP also rejected this deal, citing morality issues.

In the following days, the JKN also announced its intention

to support the PDP from outside by submitting a letter to governor Narinder Nath Vohra after the dialogue with the BJP fell through. The PDP refused. A week after the results, the PDP and the BJP officially started talks.

Both parties had a two-member team to form a Common Minimum Programme (CMP). The PDP was represented by Naeem Akhtar and Haseeb Drabu, while Ram Madhav and Nirmal Kumar Singh represented the BJP. Minister of State in the PMO, Jitendra Singh, supervised the dialogue.

Omar Abdullah resigned as chief minister on 24 December. The Governor accepted his resignation, but asked him to continue in an interim capacity until the formation of a new government. President's rule was imposed on 1 January 2015.

After dealing with issues, both parties turned their attention to the composition of the cabinet. The PDP was initially reluctant for a three-year rotation of the chief minister's post, but later agreed.

There were also issues related to the joining of the government by separatist-turned-politician Sajjad Lone. In the run-up to the election, he met Prime Minister Narendra Modi and praised him by calling him "big brother." The BJP reciprocated by not running a candidate against Lone for the Handwara seat, from where he won, and got elected to the assembly for the first time.

Both parties announced on 25 February that the CMP was almost ready, in a joint press conference called by BJP national President Amit Shah and PDP President Mehbooba Mufti. They also stated that the ideological differences had been "ironed out" and both parties were now working on the formation of a cabinet. The dialogue between both parties ended successfully on 18 February - two months and 5 days after beginning of talks.

The new PDP-BJP government took the oath of office on 1 March in the Zorawar Singh Stadium of Jammu, with Mufti Mohammad Sayeed as chief minister for the full term of six years and Nirmal Kumar Singh as his deputy. Modi was also present for the occasion. Twelve cabinet ministers from each party were also sworn-in. This was the first time that the BJP was a coalition partner in the Jammu and Kashmir government. Lone and independent MLA for Udhampur, Pawan Kumar Gupta, were also sworn-in as cabinet ministers from the BJP's quota.

The CMP was then released in a press conference. The CMP gave a vision of "all-round development of Jammu and Kashmir" and "Sabka Saath, Sabka Vikas" (with everyone, everyone's development).

Contentious issues like Article 370 and AFSPA would be referred to a high-power committee, with representation from both parties and civil society.

The PDP also agreed to join the NDA's central, with Mehbooba Mufti's induction into the union cabinet, at a later date, and also support the Modi government in both houses of parliament.

ADMINISTRATIVE DIVISIONS

Jammu and Kashmir consists of three divisions: Jammu, Kashmir Valley and Ladakh, and is further divided into 22 districts. The Siachen Glacier, although under Indian military control, does not lie under the administration of the state of Jammu and Kashmir. Kishtwar, Ramban, Reasi, Samba, Bandipora, Ganderbal, Kulgam and Shopian are newly formed districts, and their areas are included with those of the districts from which they were formed.

Major cities

Municipal corporations: 2 – Srinagar, Jammu

Municipal councils: 6 – Udhampur, Kathua, Poonch, Anantnag, Baramulla, Sopore

Municipal Committees: 70 –

Municipal boards: 21 – Samba, Ranbirsinghpora, Akhnoor, Reasi, Ramban, Doda, Bhaderwah, Kishtwar, Kargil, Dooru-Verinag, Bijbehara, Pulwama, Tral, Badgam, Kulgam, Shopian, Ganderbal, Pattan, Sumbal, Kupwara, Handwara

Population of ten major cities:

Name	Rank	Population 2011 Census	State Region
Jammu	1	1,529,958	Jammu
Srinagar	2	1,236,829	Kashmir
Anantnag	3	1,078,692	Kashmir
Baramulla	4	1,008,039	Kashmir
Udhampur	5	554,985	Jammu
Rajouri	6	642,415	Jammu
Kathua	7	616,435	Jammu
Sopore	8	-	Kashmir
Poonch	9	-	Jammu
Bandipora	10	-	Kashmir

POLITICAL PARTY OF JAMMU AND KASHMIR

All Jammu & Kashmir Patriotic Peoples Front

All Jammu & Kashmir Patriotic Peoples Front, a political party in Jammu and Kashmir. The group is a pro-Indian faction, linked to the so-called *counter-insurgents* (paramilitaries). Muslim Mujahedeen was an Islamist guerrilla group, that turned themselves in to the government in 1995 and developed cooperation with the Indian army. Muslim Mujahedeen had been formed as a splinter group of Hizb-ul-Mujahedeen in 1993. Patriotic Peoples Front was formed by Muslim Mujahedeen as a structure for contesting elections.

The forces of Muslim Mujahedeen were demobilzed around 1997-1998, but later parts of the group reorganized.

After 1997 PPF supported Farooq Abdullah's Jammu & Kashmir National Conference government in Kashmir.

In the Lok Sabha elections 1999 the leader of PPF Ghulam Nabi Mir was a candidate in the constituency of Anantnag. He got 1 500 votes (1,46%).

In 2001 the PPF leader and Muslim Mujahedeen chief commander Ghulam Nabi Mir was killed.

Democratic Janata Dal (Jammu and Kashmir)

The Democratic Janata Dal is a political party in Jammu and Kashmir. DJD had merged with the Jammu & Kashmir National Conference in 1998, but on February 3, 1999 DJD was revived as a separate party. The party president is Ghulam Qadir Wani and the general secretary is Yograj Singh.

Democratic National Conference

Democratic National Conference, a splinter group of the Jammu & Kashmir National Conference. DNC was formed by Ghulam Muhammad Sadiq in 1957. DNC later joined the Communist Party of India, then CPI(M) and then CPI(ML).

International Democratic Party

The International Democratic Party is a political party in Jammu and Kashmir in the Republic of India. The IDP was founded by R.P. Saraf.

The state secretary of the IDP is Hoshiar Singh.

The IDP favours joint Indo-Pakistani control over Kashmir as a means to achieve peace. The party also favours increased autonomy for the Jammu and Laddakh regions.

Jamaat-e-Islami Kashmir

The Jamaat-e-Islami Kashmir is the Jammu and Kashmir unit of the Islamist group, the Jamaat-e-Islami. Its organisation is distinct from the Jamaat-e-Islami Hind, the Indian branch of the Jamaat to emphasize the organisation's stance that Jammu and Kashmir is not a part of India.

Jammu & Kashmir National Conference

The Jammu & Kashmir National Conference is the largest political party in Jammu and Kashmir, India. Led at the time of Indian Independence in 1947 by Sheikh Abdullah, it has since then dominated electoral politics in the state, and was led subsequently by the Sheikh's son Farooq Abdullah and now by his son Omar Abdullah. It was defeated by a huge margin by Jammu and Kashmir Peoples Democratic Party.

Jammu & Kashmir Democratic Freedom Party

Jammu and Kashmir Democratic Freedom Party, a political party launched by separatist leader Shabir Ahmad Shah on May 25, 1998. JKDFP called for tripartite negotiations between India, Pakistan and Kashmir.

Jammu & Kashmir National Panthers Party

The Jammu & Kashmir National Panthers Party is a political party based in Jammu and Kashmir, India. It has the status of a 'state party'. Bhim Singh is the party chief.

Mallah Insaf Party

Mallah Insaf Party, a political party in Jammu and Kashmir. MIP was formed prior to the 2002 state assembly elections. Party president is Ghulam Ahmad Pardesi.

Praja Parishad Jammu & Kashmir

Praja Parishad Jammu and Kashmir (Popular Association Jammu and Kashmir) is a political party in the Indian state of Jammu and Kashmir. PP was floated by dissidents of the Bharatiya Janata Party in January 2005. The name is taken from the Praja Parishad, which fought against the special status of J&K (Article 370 of the Indian Constitution). Praja Parishad had merged with Bharatiya Jana Sangh in 1970.

The new party is led by Chandermohan Sharma. The party works for autonomy for the Jammu region within J&K.

Jammu & Kashmir People's Democratic Party

The Jammu and Kashmir People's Democratic Party is a political party in Jammu and Kashmir, India. It was founded in 1999 by the former Union Home Minister, Mufti Mohammed

Sayeed, and captured power in the state of Jammu and Kashmir in October 2002 assembly elections. Since 2004 it has one member each in the Lok Sabha and in the Rajya Sabha. It is a member of the ruling United Progressive Alliance.

Peoples Democratic Party is presently headed by Ms. Mehbooba Mufti, while Mufti Mohammad Sayeed, who headed the PDP-Congress Coalition Government between October 2002 and November 2005, is the party's Patron.

Members of Parliament

- 1977: Mohammed Shafi Qureshi, Indian National Congress
- 1980: Gh. Rasool Kochak, Jammu & Kashmir National Conference
- 1984: Akbar Jahan Begum, Jammu & Kashmir National Conference
- 1989: P.L. Handoo, Jammu & Kashmir National Conference
- 1996: Mohammad Maqbool, Janata Dal
- 1998: Mufti Mohmad Sayeed, Indian National Congress
- 1999: Ali Mohammad Naik, Jammu & Kashmir National Conference
- 2004: Mehbooba Mufti, Jammu & Kashmir People's Democratic Party

4

Language and Literature

KASHMIRI LANGUAGE

Kashmiri is a language from the Dardic subgroup of Indo-Aryan languages and it is spoken primarily by the Kashmiris in the Kashmir Valley and Chenab Valley of Jammu and Kashmir.

There are about 6.8 million speakers of Kashmiri and related dialects in Jammu and Kashmir state of India and amongst the Kashmiri diaspora in other states of India, and about 130,000 in the Neelam and Leepa valleys of Azad Kashmir, Pakistan.

The Kashmiri language is one of the 22 scheduled languages of India, and is a part of the *eighth Schedule* in the constitution of the Jammu and Kashmir. Along with other regional languages mentioned in the *Sixth Schedule*, as well as Hindi and Urdu, the Kashmiri language is to be developed in the state. Most Kashmiri speakers use Urdu or English as a second language. Since November 2008, the Kashmiri language has been made a compulsory subject in all government schools in the Valley up to secondary level.

Literature

In 1919 George Abraham Grierson wrote that "Kashmiri

is the only one of the Dardic languages that has a literature". Kashmiri literature dates back to over 750 years, this is, more-or-less, the age of many a modern literature including modern English.

Grammar

Kashmiri is a fusional language with verb-second (V2) word order. Several of Kashmiri's grammatical features distinguish it from other Indo-Aryan languages.

Nouns

Kashmiri nouns are inflected according to gender, number and case. There are no articles, nor is there any grammatical distinction for definiteness, although there is some optional adverbial marking for indefinite or "generic" noun qualities.

Gender

The Kashmiri gender system is divided into masculine and feminine. Feminine forms are typically generated by the addition of a suffix (or in most cases, a morphophonemic change, or both) to a masculine noun. There is also a relatively small group of feminine nouns that have unique suppletion forms which are totally different from the corresponding masculine forms.

Some nouns borrowed from other languages, such as Persian, Arabic, Sanskrit, Hindi or English, follow a slightly different gender system. Notably, many words borrowed from Hindi have different genders in Kashmiri.

Case

There are five cases in Kashmiri: nominative, dative, ergative, ablative and vocative. Case is expressed via suffixation of the noun.

Kashmiri utilizes an ergative-absolutive case structure when the verb is in simple past tense. Thus, in these sentences, the subject of a transitive verb is marked in the ergative case and the object in nominative, which is identical to how the subject of an intransitive verb would be marked. However, in sentences constructed in any other tense, or in past tense sentences with intransitive verbs, a nominative-dative paradigm is adopted, with objects (whether direct or indirect) generally marked in dative case.

Other case distinctions, such as locative, instrumental, genitive, comitative and allative, are marked by postpositions rather than suffixation.

Vocabulary

There are minor differences between the Kashmiri spoken by Hindus and Muslims. For 'fire', a traditional Hindu will use the word *agun* while a Muslim more often will use the Arabic word *nar*.

Preservation of old Indo-Aryan vocabulary

Kashmiri retains several features of Old Indo-Aryan that have been lost in other modern Indo-Aryan languages such as Hindi-Urdu, Punjabi and Sindhi. Some vocabulary features that Kashmiri preserves clearly date from the Vedic Sanskrit era and had already been lost even in Classical Sanskrit. This includes the word-form *yodvai* (meaning *if*), which is mainly found in Vedic Sanskrit texts. Classical Sanskrit and modern Indo-Aryan use instead the word *yadi*.

First person pronoun

Both the Indo-Aryan and Iranian branches of the Indo-Iranian family have demonstrated a strong tendency to eliminate the distinctive first person pronoun ("I") used in the nominative (subject) case. The Indo-European root for this is reconstructed as *e□Hom, which is preserved in Sanskrit as*aham* and in Avestan Persian as *azam*. This contrasts with the *m-* form ("me", "my") that is used for the accusative, genitive, dative, ablative cases. Sanskrit and Avestan both used forms such as *ma(-m)*. However, in languages such as Modern Persian, Baluchi, Hindi and Punjabi, the distinct nominative form has been entirely lost and replaced with *m-* in words such as *ma-n* and *mai*. However, Kashmiri belongs to a relatively small set that preserves the distinction.

'I' is *ba/bi/bo* in various Kashmiri dialects, distinct from the other *me* terms. 'Mine' is *myoon* in Kashmiri. Other Indo-Aryan languages that preserve this feature include Dogri (*aun* vs *me-*), Gujarati (*hu-n* vs *ma-ri*), Konkani (hə̃v vs *mhazo*), and Braj (*hau-M* vs *mai-M*). The Iranian Pashto preserves it too (*za* vs. *maa*).

LANGUAGE SPOKEN

Urdu is the official language of Jammu & Kashmir though, the local language in Jammu & Kashmir is Kashmiri.

Kashmiri is also called Koshur, and it is a language of Indo-Aryan origin. Kashmiri is the language of people living within Kashmir valley while Ladakhi is the language of those living in Ladakh and Dogri is mostly spoken by those living in Jammu.

Kashmiri Pandits and Gujjar people within the state mostly speak Hindi. Urdu that is a language of Indo-European origin is largely spoken by Muslim population within Kashmir. Urdu language is similar sounding to Hindi.

The educated class, as well as guides, within the state speak in English.

Language

- Kashmiri is considered as one amongst the 22 national languages within India.
- There are approximately more than 5 million speakers within northern regions of the country.
- This is largely spoken within the Kashmir valley in the Jammu & Kashmir administered state, where it is regarded as an official language. As many as 105,000 immigrants speak this language within Pakistan from Kashmir Valley.
- Many speakers of Kashmiri language also speak in English, Urdu and Hindi as the second language.

Area and Speakers

Native speakers call Kashmiri language ka-shir zaba-n or ka-shur. This language is mostly spoken within Kashmir Valley of Jammu & Kashmir state within India. As per the census of 1981 there are approximately 30,76,398 people who speak this language. The census for the year 1991 was not conducted. After considering an increase in population over the year, it can be predicted that the current number of speakers of this language are approximately four million. Kashmiri language is also spoken by Kashmiri people settled in other areas within India and those settled in other countries. The language spoken in neighboring areas of Srinagar is largely considered being the standard variety. The language is also used in literature, education as well as mass media.

Classification and Dialects

Historical linguists have a consensus that Kashmiri language belongs to Dardic branch of Indo-Aryan family. Kashmiri is classified under the Dardic group in Indo-Aryan languages by Grierson (1919) as well as Mogenstierne (1961) and Fussman (1972).

The Dardic t.mp3 is not considered a linguistic expression but is stated as only a geographical convention. Classification of the Kashmiri, as well as the other Dardic languages, was reviewed in certain works (Kachru in 1969 followed by Strand in 1973 and Koul and Schmidt, in 1984). This review was done with different purposes. Kachru pointed the linguistic characteristics of the Kashmiri language. Strand presented observations on the Kafir languages. Koul and Schmidt reviewed literature on classification of the Dardic languages. They also investigated linguistic characteristics or the different features of the languages with specific reference to Kashmiri as well as Shina.

Kashmiri has Two Types of Dialects

(a) Regional dialects

(b) The Social dialects.

Regional Dialects Can be Further Classified in Two Types

- The regional dialects or the variations that are spoken within regions inside the Kashmir valley
- Those dialects or variations spoken within regions that are outside the Kashmir valley.

Kashmiri Speaking Areas Within the Valley are Divided Ethno-Semantically into Three Different Regions

(1) Maraz (southern as well as the south-eastern region),

(2) Kamraz (northern & the north-western region) and

(3) Srinagar along with its neighboring areas.

There are certain minimal linguistic variations that are mostly at phonological as well as lexical levels. Kashmiri spoken within these three regions is homogeneous and completely mutually intelligible. Such dialectical variations are t.mp3ed to be different styles in the same speech. Kashmiri, spoken within and around Srinagar area has gained considerable social prestige, and so frequent 'style switching' from Kamrazi or Marazi styles to the style spoken within Srinagar and surrounding areas takes place. Such style switching phenomena is quite common, particularly among the educated speakers of the language. Kashmiri spoken within Srinagar, and other surrounding areas continues to be regarded as the standard variety that is largely used within mass media as well as literature.

Balti Language

Balti: All people of different races, living in Baltistan are called Balti. Balti is derived from the Greek name Byaltae. The historian Ptolemy who was also a general in the army of Alexander the Great had named the region (Byaltae) in his book. In fact Baltistan is the Persian translation of "The Homeland of Balti". The people belonging to Balti nationality are settled on both banks of the river Indus from Kargil (in the east) to Haramosh (in the west) and from Karakoram range (in the north) to Deosai plains (in the south). In this nationality the majority comes from Tibetan origin. However people migrated to this area in different periods of ancient times, on account of different reasons and after merging in the prevailing Tibetan society, gave birth to a new civilisation. All these multi-racial groups speak Balti language, which is a branch of the ancient Tibetan language. However in some rural areas, the SHEEN people still speak Shina language.

The Balti are a very forbearing, cheerful, and hospitable people. During the reign of the Maqpoon reign (from 12th century to 1840 A.D.) they invaded Laddakh and Tibet in the east and Gilgit and Chitral many times and thus made these people acknowledge their martial abilities. In the Liberation war of 1947 they also accomplished many memorable deeds. The well-known Padam Party performed unforgettable tasks of courage and bravery.

Script: Balti is also the name of the Tibetan Balti script, which was replaced by the Persian script in the 17th century.

Recently a number of Balti scholars and social activists are trying to repromote the use of the Balti script (Yige) which will also help to preserve indigenous Laddakhi and Balti form of culture and racial identity.

Vocabulary: The Balti language shares 90% of the vocabulary with the neighbouring Laddakhi, as well as Amdo and Kham dialect of North Eastern Tibet. However, they have adopted words from Shina, Burushaski and Persian with the process of Islamization.

Dogri Language

Dogri is an Indo-Aryan language spoken by about two million people in India and Pakistan, chiefly in the Jammu region of Jammu and Kashmir, but also in northern Punjab, Himachal Pradesh, other parts of Kashmir, and elsewhere. Dogri speakers are called Dogras, and the Dogri-speaking region is called Duggar. Dogri is a member of the Western Pahari Group of languages. The language is referred to as Pahari in Pakistan and Pakistani-administered parts of Kashmir. Unusually for an Indo-European language, Dogri is tonal, a trait it shares with other Western Pahari languages and Punjabi.

Script: Dogri was originally written using the Takri script, which is closely related to the Sharada script employed by Kashmiri and the Gurmukhi script used to write Punjabi. It is now more commonly written in Devanagari in India, and the Nasta'liq form of Perso-Arabic in Pakistan and Pakistani-administered Kashmir.

Tonality: Western Pahari languages, Punjabi and Punjabi dialects are frequently tonal, which is very unusual for Indo-European languages. This tonality makes it difficult for speakers of other Indo-Aryan languages to gain facility in Dogri, though native Punjabi speakers (especially speakers of Northern dialects such as Hindko and Mirpuri) may find it easier to make the transition. Some common examples are shown below.

Sentence	*Tone*	*English Translation*
Kora ha.	Equal	It was a whip.
Kora ha.	Falling-Rising	It was a horse.
Kora ha.	Rising	It was bitter.
Das keeyaan?	Falling	Why is it ten?
Das keeyaan.	Rising	Tell me how (it happened).

The Greek astrologer Pulomi, accompanying Alexander in his 323 B.C. campaign into the Indian subcontinent, referred to some inhabitants of Duggar as *"a brave Dogra family living in the mountain ranges of Shivalik."* [Source: (Translated from) "Dogri in the family of world languages," Balkrishan Shastri, Dogri Research-1981, Dogri Research Centre, Jammu University, Jammu].

In the year 1317, Amir Khusro, the famous poet of Hindi and Persian, referred to Duger (Dogri) while describing the languages and dialects of India as follows: *"Sindhi O' Lahori O' Kashmiri O' Duger."* [Source: (Translated from) "Dogri Prose Writing before Independence," Ram Nath Shastri, Dogri Research-1981, Dogri Research Centre, Jammu University, Jammu].

Theories on Name Origin: Intellectuals in the court of Maharaja Ranbir Singh of Jammu and Kashmir, described 'Duggar' as a distorted form of the word 'Dwigart,' which means "two troughs," a possible reference to the Mansar and Sruinsar Lakes.

The linguist Drew connected the term 'Duggar' with the Rajasthani word 'Doonger,' which means 'hill,' and 'Dogra' with 'Dongar.' This opinion has sometimes lacked support however, because of the inconsistency of the ostensible changes from Rajasthani to Dogri (essentially the question of how Doonger became Duggar while Donger became Dogra).

Yet another proposal stems from the presence of the word 'Durger' in the Bhuri Singh Museum (in Chamba, Himachal Pradesh). The word Durger means 'invincible' in several Northern Indian languages, and could be an allusion to the ruggedness of the Duggar terrain and the historically militarized and autonomous Dogra societies.

In 1976, the experts attending the Language Session of the 'All India Oriental Conference' held in Dharwar, Karnataka could not reach consensus on the 'Dwigart' and 'Durger' hypotheses, but did manage agreement on a Doonger-Duggar connection. In a subsequent 'All India Oriental Conference' held at Jaipur in 1982, the linguists agreed that the culture, language and history of Rajasthan and Duggar share some similarities. It was also suggested that the words 'Duggar' and 'Dogra' are common in some parts of Rajasthan. Specifically, it was asserted that areas with a large number of forts are called Duggar, and their inhabitants are accordingly known as Dogras. The land of Duggar also has a large number of forts, which may support the opinion above. An article by Dharam Chand Prashant in the literary magazine Shiraza Dogri suggested that *"the opinion that the word 'Duggar' is a form of the word 'Duggarh' sounds appropriate."* ["Duggar Shabad di Vayakha," Dharam Chand Prashant, Shiraza Dogri, April-May 1991, Jammu and Kashmir Academy of Arts, Culture and Languages]

Recent History: In modern times, a notable Dogri translation (in the Takri script) of the Sanskrit classic mathematical opus "Lilavati," by the noted mathematician Bhaskaracharya (b. 1114 A.D.), was published by the Vidya Vilas Press, Jammu in 1873. As Sanskrit literacy remained confined to a few, the late Kashmiri Maharaja Ranbir Singh had the *Lilavati* translated into Dogri by Jyotshi Bisheshwar, then principal of Jammu Pathshala. (Ref. : Century Old Printed Dogri, Literature by B. P. Sharma, Jammu & Kashmir State Research Biannual)

Dogri has an established tradition of poetry, fiction and dramatic works. Recent poets range from the 18th century Dogri poet Kavi Dattu (1725-1780) in Raja Ranjit Dev's court to Professor Ram Nath Shastri and Mrs. Padma Sachdev. Kavi Dattu is highly regarded for his Barah Massa (Twelve Months), Kamal Netra (Lotus Eyes), Bhup Bijog and Bir Bilas. Shiraza Dogri is a Dogri literary periodical issued by the Jammu and Kashmir Academy of Art, Culture and Languages, which is a notable publisher of modern Dogri literary work, another being the Dogri Sanstha. Popular recent songs include *Pala Shpaiya Dogarya*, *Manney di Mauj* and *Shhori Deya*. The noted Pakistani singer Malika Pukhraj had roots in the Duggar region and her renditions of several Dogri songs continue to be popular in the region. Some devotional songs, or bhajans, composed by Karan Singh have gained increasing popularity over time, including *Kaun Kareyaan Teri Aarti*.

Dogri programming features regularly on Radio Kashmir (a division of All India Radio) and Doordarshan (Indian state television) broadcasts in Jammu and Kashmir. However, Dogri does not have a dedicated state television channel yet, unlike Kashmiri (which has the Doordarshan Koshur channel, available on cable and satellite television throughout India).

Official recognition of the language has been gradual, but progressive. On 2nd August 1969, the General Council of the Sahitya Academy, Delhi recognized Dogri as an "independent modern literary language" of India, based on the unanimous recommendation of a panel of linguists. (Indian Express, New Delhi, 3rd August, 1969). Dogri is one of the state languages of the Indian state of Jammu and Kashmir. On 22 December 2003, in a major milestone for the official status of the language, Dogri was recognized as a national language of India in the Indian constitution. In Pakistan, the language (under the name "Pahari") continues to thrive, but is not known to have received official patronage to date. The Alami Pahari Adabi Sangat (Global Pahari Cultural Association) is a Pakistani organization dedicated to the advancement and progress of the language.

Language and Dialects: Since Dogri, Kashmiri, Punjabi, Urdu and Hindi are spoken in a region that has witnessed significant ethnic and identity conflict, all have been exposed to the dialect versus language question. At various times, Western Pahari languages have been contended to be dialects of Punjabi, at others, some Western Pahari languages (such as Rambani) have been contended to be dialects of Kashmiri.

Similarly, Punjabi has been held to be a dialect of Hindi by many Hindi-speakers. To some extent, "a language is a dialect with an army and navy." In modern linguistics, Hindi, Urdu, Punjabi, Kashmiri and Dogri are each considered a distinct Indo-Iranian language. Each of these languages possesses a central standard on which its literature is based, and from which there are multiple dialectical variations.

Kashmiri Language

Kashmiri is a northern Indo-Aryan language spoken primarily in the valley of Kashmir, a region situated mostly in the Indian Jammu and Kashmir state. It has about 4,611,000 speakers. While Kashmiri belongs to the Indo-Aryan branch of the Indo-European family of languages it is sometimes placed in a geographical sub-grouping called Dardic. It is one of the 23 officially recognised languages of India.

It is a V2 word order language. Kashmiri has remained a spoken language up to the present times, though some manuscripts were written in the past in the Sharada script, and then in Perso-Arabic script. Currently, Kashmiri is written in either the Perso-Arabic script (with some modifications) or the Devanagari script. The earliest literary composition in Kashmiri that has survived is the poetry of Lalleshvari, a 14th century mystic poetess.

Literacy in Kashmiri is continuously neglected due to various political reasons and lack of formal education in it. It is now mostly relevant in its spoken form, and the speakers of this language are also decreasing in number. Note that the primary official language of the state of Jammu and Kashmir is not Kashmiri, but Urdu. In the past few decades, Kashmiri was introduced as a subject at the university and the colleges of the valley. At present, attempts are on for inclusion of Kashmiri in school curriculum.

There is only one online newspaper in Kashmiri, though a number of literary magazines are published regularly.

The Kashmiri language has a rich literary heritage. It has been the language of numerous sufi and folk poets. The songs in the Kashmiri language are called *gewun* /gewun/ and the chorus songs are known as *wonwun* /wonwun/.

Vast majorities of People of the Kashmiri origin are spread over the whole state in the disputed territory; but the majority is living in valley of Kashmir, Kishtwar, Badarwah, Doda and Ramban. The majority of Kashmiris follow the Islamic faith. However, other minorities such as Hindus, Sikhs, and Christians introduced by the British Colonist are also found among them. Kashmiris living in rural areas are agriculturists while those living in cities and towns are associated with different trades industries and handicrafts. Kashmiri is their common language that is also spoken in some areas of Poonch and Muzaffarabad.

Oppressed Kashmiris are divided into many sub-castes, which include Sheikhs, Sayids, Mughals, Pathans, etc. Butts, Koals, Pandits, Yatus, Rishis, Mantoos, Ganayis and Kichloos are believed to be from Brahman casts whereas Magrays, Dars, Thakurs, and Naiks are believed to be Khishtris. Lones are from the vesh caste and Damars are from Shudar caste. Kashmiri Mughals add to their names Mir, Mirza, or Baig. Ashayees and Bandays are also from the Mughals origin. The majority of Hindus comprise of Brahmans which include Razadan,

Kak, Raina, Sapru, Kol, Zatshi, Nehru, Butt, Kachru, Kachlu etc... pundit is added to all of these such as Pundit Ramchand Kak, and Pandit Jawarlal Nehru. Historian Bamzai has quated 133 sub-castes of Brahmins in Occupied Kashmir.

Laddakhi Language

The Laddakhi language is the predominant language in the Laddakh region of the Jammu and Kashmir state of India. Laddakhi is closely related to Tibetan, and the Laddakh people share cultural similarities with Tibetans, including Tibetan Buddhism. Laddakhi has approximately 100,000 speakers in India, and perhaps 12,000 speakers in the Tibet region of China. Laddakhi has several dialects, Laddakhi proper (also called after the capital of Laddakh, Leh, where it is spoken); Shamma, spoken to the northwest of Leh; Stopta, spoken to the south east in the Indus alley; Nubra, spoken in the north. A variant of Laddakhi is also spoken by some in Zanskar. Laddakhi is romanised in a similar way to Hindi, 'th' denoting an aspirated 't,' for example.

Script: Laddakhi is usually written using Tibetan script. The phenomenon of diglossia is very much present in Laddakhi, with written Laddakhi being much closer to Tibetan proper.

Shina Language

Tshina or Shina is a Dardic Language and is spoken by majority of people in Northern Areas of Pakistan. The Valleys include Astore, Chilas, Dareil, Tangeer, Gilgit, Ghizer, and few parts of Baltistan, and Kohistan. It is also spoken in Kargil and Laddakh valleys of India. There are 321,000 speakers.

LITERATURE OF KASHMIR

Literature of Kashmir has a long history, the oldest texts having been composed in the Sanskrit language. Early names include Patanjali, the author of the *Mahabhashya*commentary on PâG□ini's grammar, suggested by some to have been the same to write the Hindu treatise known as the Yogasutra, and Dridhbala, who revised the Charaka Samhitaof Ayurveda.

In medieval times, philosophers of Kashmir Shaivism include Vasugupta (c. 800), Utpala (c. 925), Abhinavagupta, and Kshemaraja as well as Anandavardhana.

Kashmiri language literature

The use of the Kashmiri language began with the work *Mahanayakaprakash* (Light of the Supreme Lord) by Shitikantha (c.1250), and was followed by the poet Lalleshvari or Lal Ded (14th century), who wrote mystical verses in the *vakh* or four-line couplet style. Another mystic of her time equally revered in Kashmir and popularly known as Nund Reshiwrote powerful poetry. Later came Habba Khatun (16th century) with her own style. Other major names are Rupa Bhavani (1621–1721), Arnimal (d. 1800), Mahmud Gami (1765–1855), Rasul Mir (d. 1870), Paramananda (1791–1864), Maqbool Shah Kralawari (1820–1876). Also, the Sufi poets like Shamas Fakir, Wahab Khar, Soch Kral, Samad Mir, and Ahad Zargar. Among modern poets are Ghulam Ahmad Mahjur (1885–1952), Abdul Ahad Azad (1903–1948), and Zinda Kaul (1884–1965).

During the 1950s, a number of well educated youth turned to Kashmiri writing, both poetry and prose, and enriched modern Kashmiri writing by leaps and bounds. Among these writers are Dinanath Nadim (1916–1988), Rahman Rahi, Ghulam Nabi Firaq Amin Kamil (1923-2014), Ali Mohd Lone, Autar Krishen Rahbar (born 1933), Akhtar Mohiuddin, Sajood Sailani (brn 1933), Som Nath Zutshi, Muzaffar Aazim, and Sarwanand Kaol Premi. Some later day writers are Hari Krishan Kaul, Majrooh Rashid, Rattanlal Shant, Hirdhey Kaul Bharti, Omkar N Koul, Roop Krishen Bhat, Rafiq Raaz, Tariq Shehraz, Shafi Shauq, Showkat Shehri, M H Zaffar, Shenaz Rashid, Shabir Ahmad Shabir, Shabir Magami, and Moti Lal Kemmu.

Contemporary Kashmiri literature appears in such magazines as *Sheeraza* published by the Jammu & Kashmir Academy of Art, Culture and Languages, *Anhar* published by the Kashmirri Department of the Kashmir University, and an independent magazine *Neab International Kashmiri Magazine* published from Boston, *Vaakh* (published by All India Kashmiri Samaj, Delhi) and *Koshur Samachar* (published by Kashmiri Sahayak Sammiti, Delhi).

Ancient writers in Sanskrit

- Lagadha, between 1400-1200 BC. Wrote Vedanga Jyotisha, the earliest Indian text on astronomy.
- Charaka, c. 300 BC. One of the most important authors in Ayurveda.
- Vishnu Sharma, c. 300 BC. Author of Panchatantra.
- Nagasena, c. 2nd century BC. One of the major figures of Buddhism, his answers to questions about the religion posed by Menander I (Pali: Milinda), the Indo-Greek king of northwestern India (now Pakistan), are recorded in the *Milinda Pañha.*
- Tisata, c. 500 AD. A medical writer.
- Jaijjata, 5th century, a medical writer and probably the earliest commentator (known) on the Sushruta Samhita, later quoted by Dalhana.
- Kalidasa, c. 5th century. Widely regarded as the greatest poet and dramatist in the Sanskrit language.
- Vagbhata, c. 7th century. Considered as one of the 'trinity' (with Charaka and Sushruta) of Ayurveda.
- Bhamaha, c. 7th century
- Ravigupta, 700-725. "Ravigupta is, perhaps, the earliest among the Buddhist philosophers of Kashmir..."
- Anandavardhana, 820-890
- Vasugupta, 860-925
- Somananda, 875-925
- Vatesvara, b. 880, author of Vam□eúvara-siddhânta.
- Rudrata, c. 9th century
- Jayanta Bhatta, c. 9th century
- Bhatta Nayaka, c. 9th-10th century, considered by Sheldon Pollock as the greatest author on aesthetics in the pre-modern period

- Medhâtithi, c. 9th-10th century, one of the most influential commentators of the Manusmriti
- Utpaladeva, 900-950
- Abhinavagupta, c. 950-1020
- Vallabhadeva, c. 10th century. Wrote, amongst other works, *Raghupanchika*, the earliest commentary on the *Raghuvamsa* of Kalidasa.
- Utpala, c. 10th century. An important mathematician.
- Kshemendra, c. 990-1070
- Kshemaraja, c. late 10th century/early 11th century
- Kathasaritsagara, c. 11th century
- Bilhana, c. 11th century
- Kalhana, c. 12th century
- Jalhana, c. 12th century, the author of *Mugdhopadesa* (not to be confused with Jalhana who commissioned the *Suktimuktavali*)
- Sarangadeva, c. 13th century. A musicologist, he wrote Sangita Ratnakara, one of the most important text when it comes to Indian music.
- Kesava Kashmiri Bhattacharya, c. 14th century, a major Vedantic philosopher.
- Mamatta
- Kaihata
- Jaihata
- Ralhana
- Shilhana
- Malhana
- Ruiyaka
- Kuntaka
- Ruchaka
- Udbhatta
- Sankuka
- Gunadhya

- Somvadeva
- Pingala
- Jayadata
- Vamana
- Kshiraswamin
- Mankha
- Pushpadanta
- Jagadhar Bhatta
- Ratnakara
- Manikyacandra

Writers in Persian

After Sanskrit and before the coming Urdu, because of the adoration and patronising policy of foreign culture by the Mughals, Persian became the literary language also of the region. Kashmir was very richly represented in that tradition, as already before the end of the 18th century "Muhammad Aslah's tazkira of the Persian-writing poets of Kashmir, written during the reign of the Mughal emperor Muhammad Shah (1131-61/1719-48), alone lists 303 poets". Late scholar from Pakistan, Pir Hassam-ud-Din Rashidi, edited, translated, and enlarged this work later, and had it published by the Iqbal Academy.

The most famous of them was Muhammad Tahir Ghani (d. 1669), better known as Ghani Kashmiri, whose poetry was recently translated into English, for the first time, by Mufti Mudasir Farooqi and Nusrat Bazaz as 'The Captured Gazelle' in the world-renowned Penguin Classics list. Ghani influenced many generations of Persian-and Urdu writing poets in South Asia including Mir Taqi Mir, Ghalib and most importantly, Iqbal. Ghani's "forte" lies in creating delightful poetic images, usually by stating an abstract idea in the first hemistich and following it up with a concrete exemplification in the other. He also stands out for his multi-layered poems, which exploit the double meaning of words.

Another name is the Sheikh Yaqub Sarfi (1521-1595), a 16th-century Sufi poet-philosopher who was internationally acknowledged and who had for students, amongst others, well-known religious scholar Ahmad Sirhindi (more particularly, he taught him hadith) and Persian-language poet Mohsin Fani Kashmiri (d. 1671 or 1672) (himself the teacher of Ghani Kashmiri and author of the pivotal work of comparative religion, the Dabestan-e Mazaheb).

Other of the well-known and influential Persian-language poets of Kashmir would include Habibullah Ghanai (1556-1617), Mirza Dirab Big Juya (d. 1707), Mirza Beg Akmal Kamil (1645-1719), Muhammad Aslam Salim (d. 1718), Mulla Muhammad Taufiq (1765), Muhammed Azam Didamari (d. 1765), Mulla Muhammad Hamid (1848) or Birbal Kachru Varasta (d. 1865), amongst a myriad. Of course, Kashmiri Pandits too played a role in that school, and one exceptional case was Pandit Taba Ram Turki (1776–1847), who was a celebrity as far as Central Asia.

Writers in Urdu

Despite being a numerically reduced community (less than one million), the Kashmiri Pandits are over-represented in their contribution to Urdu literature. One important early example is Daya Shankar Kaul Nasim (1811–1845), a renowned Urdu poet of the 19th century, and hundreds of others followed his path.

Some eminent Urdu literary personalities of Kashmiri origins (from both the Valley and the diaspora) include (in chronological order):

- Mir Tafazzul Hussain Khan Kashmiri (1727-1800), originally from Kashmir, born in Sialkot where his parents moved and himself based in Lucknow where he served as Prime Minister (or *diwan*) to the Nawab of Oudh Asaf-ud-Daula thanks his erudition. He was called "khan-e-allama" (the Scholarly Khan) due to his deep scholarship on many subjects but is best known today for having translated Sir

Isaac Newton's Philosophiæ Naturalis Principia Mathematica from Latin into Arabic.

- Mufti Sadruddin Khan 'Azurda', 1789-1868, apart from being the Grand Mufti of Dehli, he was also a personal friend to Ghalib (whose own mother was from Kashmir) and himself a poet of note in Urdu as well as in Arabic and Persian. He also wrote a *tazkira* (biographical anthology of poets).
- Momin Khan Momin, 1801-1852, considered one of the three pillars of the Delhi school of Urdu poetry, with Ghalib and Zauq. Other fields where he was competent included mathematics, geomancy, astrology, chess or music.
- Daya Shankar Kaul Nasim, 1811–1845
- Ratan Nath Dhar Sarshar, 1846-1903
- Brij Mohan Datatriya Kaifi, 1866-1955
- Muhammad Iqbal, 1877–1938
- Agha Hashar Kashmiri, 1879–1935 (called "the Shakespeare of Urdu" for his works as playwright)
- Brij Narayan Chakbast, 1882–1926
- Aziz Lucknawi, 1882-1935
- Khalifa Abdul Hakim, 1896-1959 (a philosopher who has the honour of writing the only book on the metaphysics of Persian mystical poet Jalaluddin Rumi)
- Patras Bokhari, 1898–1958
- Ghulam Mustafa Tabassum, 1899–1978
- Justice Anand Narain Mulla, 1901-1997
- Muhammad Din Taseer, 1902-1950 (short-story writer, literary critic and Iqbal scholar. Father of slain Pakistan's Punjab governor Salman Taseer and first individual from the Sub-continent to get a PhD in English Literature from Cambridge University)
- Shaikh Abdullah, 1905–1982
- Bashir Ahmed Dar, 1908-1979 (a philosopher and Iqbal scholar)

- Meeraji, 1912-1949
- Saadat Hasan Manto, 1912–1955
- Aariz Kashmiri, 1916-1965
- Agha Shorish Kashmiri, 1917-1975
- Zaheer Kashmiri, 1919-1996
- Razia Butt, 1924-2012
- Anwar Shemza, 1928-1985
- Hakeem Manzoor, 1937–2006
- Obaidullah Aleem, 1939-2008
- Muhammed Amin Andrabi, 1940-2001, a scholar who belonged to the Traditionalist School of metaphysics, inspired by authors like Ibn Arabi, Muhammad Iqbal, Frithjof Schuon, Seyyed Hossein Nasr and Henry Corbin.
- Allama Mustafa Hussain Ansari, 1945–2006
- Mirza Muhammad Zaman Azurdah, b. 1945, influential contemporary writer from the Valley
- Abid Hassan Minto
- Muhammad Asim Butt
- Muhammad Younis Butt, writer of the most popular political satire show in Pakistan, *Hum Sub Umeed Se Hain*
- Rasheed Amjad
- Shahid Nadeem

Writers in Hindi

- Amar Nath Kak
- Chandrakanta (author)
- Omkar N. Koul
- Rattan Lal Shant
- Hari Krishen Kaul
- Shashi Shekhar Toshkhani
- Bhushan Lal Koul
- Shiban Krishen Raina

- Agnishekher
- Maharaj Krishan Santoshi

Writers in English

- I. K. Taimni
- M. P. Pandit, prolific writer who authored some 150 books and as many articles exposing in English the thought of Sri Aurobindo.
- Chiragh Ali, reformist Islamic scholar
- Taufiq Rafat, called the 'Ezra Pound of Pakistan' for both his innovative writings and his position as one of - if not the - greatest English-language poets of Pakistan.
- Jawaharlal Nehru
- Vijaya Lakshmi Pandit
- Krishna Hutheesing
- Gopi Krishna
- Gopinath Raina
- Ram Nath Kak
- Subhash Kak
- Nayantara Sahgal
- M.J. Akbar
- Salman Rushdie
- Hari Kunzru
- Kailas Nath Kaul
- Agha Shahid Ali
- Mohammad Tabish
- Basharat Peer
- Hamid Naseem Rafiabadi, contemporary philosopher, affiliated with the University of Kashmir, specialist of Islamic philosophy

- Abdur Rashid Bhat, contemporary philosopher, affiliated with the University of Kashmir, specialist of al Ghazali and Shah Waliullah
- Showkat Ahmad Wani

A srinagar based poet and writer belongs to bandipora dachigam. Well known for blank verse and Urdu nazm.

KASHMIRI LITERATURE

Kashmiri literature has a history of at least 2,500 years, going back to its glory days of Sanskrit. Early names include Patanjali, the author of the *Mahabhashya* commentary on Panini's grammar, suggested by some to have been the same to write the Hindu treatise known as the Yogasutra, and Dridhbala, who revised the Charaka Samhita of Ayurveda.

In medieval times the great Hindu school of Kashmir Shaivism arose. Its great masters include Vasugupta (c. 800), Utpala (c. 925), Abhinavagupta and Kshemaraja. In the theory of aesthetics one can list the Anandavardhana and Abhinavagupta.

The use of the Kashmiri language began with the poet Lalleshvari or Lal Ded (14th century), who wrote mystical verses. Another mystic of her time equally revered in Kashmir and popularly known as Nunda Reshi wrote powerful poetry like his senoir Lal Ded. Later, came Habba Khatun (16th century) with her *lol* style. Other major names are Rupa Bhavani (1621-1721), Arnimal (d. 1800), Mahmud Gami (1765-1855), Rasul Mir (d. 1870), Paramananda(1791-1864), Maqbool Shah Kralawari (1820-1976). Also the Sufi poets like Shamas Fakir, Wahab Khar, Soch Kral, Samad Mir, and Ahad Zargar. Among modern poets are Ghulam Ahmad Mahjur (1885-1952), Abdul Ahad Azad (1903-1948), and Zinda Kaul (1884-1965).

During 1950s, a number of well educated youth turned to Kashmiri writing, both poetry and prose, and enriched modern Kashmiri writing by leaps and bounds. Among these writers are Dinanath Nadim (1916-1988), Rahman Rahi, Ghulam Nabi Firaq,

Amin Kamil (1923-:, Ali Mohd Lone, Akhtar Mohiuddin and Sarvanand Kaul 'Premi'. Some later day writers are Hari Krishan Kaul, Rattanlal Shant, Hirdhey Kaul Bharti, Moti Lal Kemmu (1933-), playwright.

Contemporary Kashmiri literature appears in Sheeraza published by the Jammu & Kashmir Academy of Art, Culture and Languages, Anhar published by the Kashmirri Department of the Kashmir University, and an independent magazine Neab International Kashmiri Magazine— published from Boston, Vaakh an independent publication and Koshur Samachar.

5

Geography and Flora & Fauna

GEOGRAPHY OF JAMMU AND KASHMIR

Jammu and Kashmir is home to several valleys such as the Kashmir Valley, Tawi Valley, Chenab Valley, Punch Valley, Sind Valley and Lidder Valley.

Nageen Lake

Lake Tso Moriri in Ladakh.

River rafting in the Zanskarsubdistrict of Kargil.

The main Kashmir valley is about 100 km (62 mi) wide and 15,520.3 km^2 (5,992.4 sq mi) in area. The Himalayas divide the

Kashmir valley from Ladakh while the Pir Panjal range, which encloses the valley from the west and the south, separates it from the Great Plains of northern India.

Along the northeastern flank of the Valley runs the main range of the Himalayas. This densely settled and beautiful valley has an average height of 1,850 metres (6,070 ft) above sea-level but the surrounding Pir Panjal range has an average elevation of 5,000 metres (16,000 ft).

The Jhelum River is the only major Himalayan river which flows through the Kashmir valley. The Indus, Tawi, Ravi and Chenab are the major rivers flowing through the state. Jammu and Kashmir is home to several Himalayan glaciers. With an average altitude of 5,753 metres (18,875 ft) above sea-level, the Siachen Glacier is 70 km (43 mi) long making it the longest Himalayan glacier.

The climate of Jammu and Kashmir varies greatly owing to its rugged topography. In the south around Jammu, the climate is typically monsoonal, though the region is sufficiently far west to average 40 to 50 mm (1.6 to 2 inches) of rain per months between January and March. In the hot season, Jammu city is very hot and can reach up to 40 °C (104 °F) whilst in July and August, very heavy though erratic rainfall occurs with monthly extremes of up to 650 millimetres (25.5 inches). In September, rainfall declines, and by October conditions are hot but extremely dry, with minimal rainfall and temperatures of around 29 °C (84 °F).

Across from the Pir Panjal range, the South Asian monsoon is no longer a factor and most precipitation falls in the spring from southwest cloudbands. Because of its closeness to the Arabian Sea, Srinagar receives as much as 25 inches (635 millimetres) of rain from this source, with the wettest months being March to May with around 85 millimetres (3.3 inches) per month. Across from the main Himalaya Range, even the southwest cloudbands break up and the climate of Ladakh and Zanskar is extremely dry and cold. Annual precipitation is only around 100 mm (4 inches) per year and humidity is very low.

This region, almost all above 3,000 metres (9,750 ft) above sea level and winters are extremely cold. In Zanskar, the average January temperature is -20 °C (-4 °F) with extremes as low as -40 °C (-40 °F). All the rivers freeze over and locals actually do river crossings during this period because their high levels from glacier melt in summer inhibits crossing. In summer in Ladakh and Zanskar, days are typically a warm 20 °C (68 °F) but with the low humidity and thin air nights can still be cold.

CLIMATE

The state of Jammu and Kashmir stretches between 32.17° to 36.58° north and the altitude rises steeply from 305 metres to 6910 metres above sea level. There are the hot plains of the Jammu Province and coldest dry tableland of Laddakh. The area has different weather conditions at different places because of the lofty mountains like the Pir Panjal, the Zanskar and the Karakoram that check the moisture-laden from entering the valleys.

In summers, the outer plains and the outer hills receive rainfall from monsoon winds while in winters, winds from the Mediterranean cause snowfall and rainfall in the Valley of Kashmir. The moisture-laden winds cause rainfall in the forests on the hills making the temperature to fall in summer; hence, the thickly wooded areas such as Pahalgam and Gulmarg have milder weather conditions than that of Srinagar or Sopore. Similarly, the climate of the valley of Kashmir is comparatively milder than that of the Outer Plains as it is on higher altitude.

The unique climatic conditions found in the zone of the Middle Mountains and its valleys, are determined by the altitude, which in turn determines the degree of coolness and elevation the form of precipitation and summer temperature. Winters are cold and of long duration and with increasing altitude, it gets colder still, till there is snowfall in the higher mountains. Summers, however, are milder but are very short. Winters last from November to March. Spring begins after 15th of March and there is heavy rainfall during the season. Landslides often take place during this season. Humidity in the monsoon season stretching over July and August is as high as 70% and with increasing temperature in summers can be uncomfortable. During this season, the entire valley is covered with a thick fog blocking the surrounding mountains from view.

Historical Background: Geologists believe that about ten crore years have passed when Kashmir Valley which was once a lake called Satisar, the lake of goddess Sati, came into its present form.

For hundreds of million years Kashmir Valley remained under Tethya Sea and the high sedimentary-rock hills seen in the valley now were once under water. Geologists have come to believe that Kashmir Valley was earlier affected by earthquakes. Once there was such a devastating earthquake that it broke open the mountain wall at Baramulla and the water of the Satisar lake flowed out leaving behind lacustrine mud on the margins of the mountains known as karewas. Thus came into existance the oval but irregular Valley of Kashmir. The karewas being in fact the remanants of this lake confirm this view. The karewas are found mostly to the west of the river Jhelum where these tablelands attain a height of about 380 meters above the level of the Valley. These karewas protrude towards the east and look like tongue-shaped spurs with deep ravines.

Ancient legends and popular traditions say that Samdimat Nagar, capital of the kingdom of Sundra Sena, was submerged as a result of an earthquake and the water that filled the area formed the Wular Lake, the largest fresh water lake in India. The oldest igneous rocks are still found at Shankaracharya hill. When the whole Valley of Kashmir was under waterthis hillock was the first piece of dry land lying in the form of an igneous island.

Significance of its Name: Historians say that Kashmir Valley was originally known as Kashyapmar or the abode of Kashyap Rishi. It is said that the Rishi once went on a pilgrimage to Kashmir. When he reached Naukabandan near Kaunsarnag via Rajouri, he killed Bahudev, the Giant of Satisar, at the request of the people and let the water of the lake flow out near Baramulla.

The land, therefore, came to be known as Kashyampar, which afterwards changed into Kashmar and from Kashmar to Kashmir. But some historians are of the opinion that when the people of Kash caste settled here permanently the valley came to be known as Kashmir. Kashmir is known by many other names also. The Greeks called it Kaspeiria, while the Chinese named it Shie-in or Kia-Shi-Lo. The Tibetans called its Kanapal and Dards named it Kashart.

Situation, Location, Area and Extent

The territories of Jammu, Kashmir, Laddakh and Gilgit form the State of Jammu and Kashmir. The state of Jammu and Kashmir, which had earlier been under Hindu rulers and Muslim sultans, became part of the Mughal Empire under Akbar from 1586. After a period of Afgan rule from 1756, it was annexed to the Sikh Kingdom of Punjab in 1819. In 1820 Maharaja Ranjit Singh made over the territory of Jammu to Gulab Singh. In 1846 Kashmir was also made over to Gulab Singh under the Treaty of Amritsar. Laddakh was annexed by Maharaja Gulab Singh in 1830. Thus this northernmost state was founded by Maharaja Gulab Singh in 1846 and was the biggest princely state in India before the partition of the country in August 1947. At that time the total area of the state was 2, 22, 236 sq. km. Pakistan invaded the State in October 1947. Indian forces pushed Pakistan back but in 1949 when a cease fire line was drawn about one third of the area *i.e.* 78932 sq. km. *i.e.* the whole of Gilgit, Mirpur, Kotli and a part of Poonch came into the possession of Pakistan, leaving behind only 143,30 sq. km. on the Indian side. Jammu, Udhampur, Kathua and Anantnag districts remained unaffected. Again in 1962 China occupied about 64000 sq.kms. in Laddakh known as Aksai Chin. Pakistan again made an unlawful possession over Chhamb, Deva, Chakla and Manawar gaining an area of 3999 sq. kms. Thus total area left on the Indian side is about 12850 sq. kms. There are many low lying valleys in the state like Tawi Valley, Chenab Valley, Poonch Valley, Sindh Valley and Liddar Valley, but the main Valley is the valley of Kashmir, which is 100 kms wide and 15520.3 sq. kms. in area. Through this velley flows the river Jhelum with its tributaries. The height of the valley above sea level is about 1700 metres.

On the map of India, the State of Jammu and Kashmir looks like a crown. The state is 640 kms. in length from north to south and 480 kms. form east to west. To its north lie Chinese and Russian Turkistan. On its east is Chinese Tibet. On the South and South-West lie the states of Punjab and Himachal Pradesh.

On the west is the North West Frontier Provinces of Pakistan, China and Russia. Afghanistan and Pakistan now have come close to the boundaries of the state of Jammu and Kashmir, The nearness to the boundaries of foreign countries has made the position of the State most important from military point of view.

The entire State lies between 32.17" and 36.58" North altitude and East to West, the State lies between 73.26" and 80.30" longitude. The standared time is 5.30 hours ahead of Greenwitch time as in the rest of India and has a difference of half an hour with the local time. In lalitude, the State of Jammu and Kashmir corresponds with South Carolina (North America), Fez (Morracco), Damascus, Baghdad and Peshawar (Pakistan).

Geographical and Political Importance of the State

Geographical Importance: Kashmir is famous for its beauty and natural scenery throughout the world. Its high snow-clad mountains, scenic spots, beautiful valleys, rivers with ice-cold water, attractive lakes and springs and evergreen fields, dense forests and beautiful health resorts, enhance its grandeur and are a source of great attraction for tourists.

It is also widely known for its different kinds of agricultural products, fruit, vegetables, saffron, herbs, minerals, precious stones handicrafts like woollen carpets, shawls and finest kind of embroidery on clothes. During summer, one can enjoy the beauty of nature, trout fishing, big and small game hunting etc.; during winter climbing mountain peaks and sports like skating and skiing on snow slopes are commonly enjoyed. In addition to the above, Pilgrimage to famous religious shrines of the Hindus and the Muslims make Kashmir a great tourist attraction. About Kashmir Sheikh Sadia great Persian poet is believed to have said said, "If there is any heaven on earth, it is here in Kashmir."

Political Importance: The state of Jammu and Kashmir has acquired since the 19th century a unique geo-political status in the Indian subcontinent It has contiguous boundaries with Russia, Afghanistan, Pakistan, China and Tibet that deserve constant vigil and as such it has made the State very important. geographically, politically, economically and from the military point of view. Jammu and Kashmir state acceded to the Indian Union in 1947 after the partition. Before the partition in 1947, The English rulers of India took away Gilgit in 1946 from the Maharaja of Jammu and Kashmir on lease for thirty years so that they could check the advancement of Russia towards India.

Physical Divisions, Mountains and Passes

The State of Jammu and Kashmir falls in the great north-western, complex of the Himalayan ranges with marked relief variation, snow- capped summits, antecedent drainage, complex geological structure and rich temperate flora and fauna.

Kashmir or the Jhelum Valley is situated between the Pir Panjal range and the Zanskar range and has an area of 15220 sq. kms. It is bounded on all sides by mountains. The river Jhelum, which flows out from the spring at Verinag in Anantnag district, passes through this Valley at a very slow speedand ultimately flows out through a narrow gorge at Baramulla. Districts of Srinagar, Anantnag, Baramulla, Kupwara and Pulwama lie in this valley. Average height of the valley is 1850 metres above sea level but the surrounding mountains, which are always snow-clad, rise from three to four thousand metres above sea level. The surface of the valley is plain and abounds with springs, lakes and health resorts.

Rice is the main crop and fruits like apples, pears, apricots, almonds, walnuts, peaches and cherries grow in abundance. The valley is also rich in forests. Mulberry trees grow in abundance and are the mainstay of silk industry in the Valley.

Summer is pleasant but winter is cold and there is snowfall. It rains from the middle of March to the middle of May in the valley with an annual rainfall of about 75 cms.

Road transport is common in the valley but the river Jhelum still serves as one of the means of transportation. There is also Air Service from Delhi and Jammu to Srinagar and Laddakh.

Kashmir is the home of handicrafts like wood carving, papier-mache, carpet, gabba and shawl making and embroidery on clothes. Natural scenery of the valley attracts thousands of visitors every year from abroad. People generally speak Kashmiri and their common dress is phiran, shalwar and a turban or a Kashmiri cap.

There are also some small valleys in this region. On the north of Baramulla is Lolab valley which is 6 Kms long and 4.4 Kms wide. It has many meadows and grovesof walnut trees. Forests are so thick that they hide villages in them.

Nullah Sindh is the largest tributory of the river Jhelum. The Nullah Sindh valley is 100 Kms long upwards and its scenery is diversified. At the head of the valley is the Zojilla pass which leads to Laddakh.

Towards Pehlgam lies the Lidar Valley. Its length is 64 Kms. It has small glaciers, grassy meadows, huge rock walls and gorges in its upper mountains. The path to the holy Amarnath cave passethrough this valley. The Kolohai and Sheshnag streams join at Pahalgam to form the Lidar river.

Mountains and their Passes: Mountains have a special geographical importance to the State of Jammu and Kashmir.

Kashmir valley is enclosed by high mountain-chains on all sides except for certain passes and a narrow gorge at Baramulla. There are Shiwalik hills towards the south and very lofty mountains in the north, the peaks of which always remain covered with snow. There are volcanic mountains too in the State. They have caused havoc in Kashmir in the past.

Some of the famous mountains and their passes are:

1. *Karakoram (8615.17 M) and Kyunlun Ranges:* Both these mountains lie to the north and northeast of the State and separate it from Russian Turkistan and Tibet. In the north west, Hindukush range continues towards Karakoram range, where K2 peak, the second highest peak of the world, is situated. Two lofty peaks of Gashorbram (8570 metres) and Masharbram (7827 metres) also lie there. People of Laddakh pass through Karakoram pass (5352 metres) and Nubra pass (5800 metres) while going to Chinese Turkistan and Khattan. One can reach Tibet from Laddakh via Kharudangala pass (5557 metres) and Changla pass (5609 metres).
2. *Zanskar Range:* It is about 600 metres above sea level and separates Indus Valley from the valley of Kashmir; it prevents southwest cold winds from reaching Kashmir. Laddakh region terminates at Zojila pass (3529 metres) from where begins the valley of Kashmir. Poat pass (5716 metres) of this range is also a famous pass in this range.
3. *Nun Kun Range:* It lies between Laddakh and kashmir border. It is 7055.1 metres above sea level. To its southeast is situated Kulu and to its northwest is situated Kargil tehsil of Laddakh. One has to pass through Bawalocha pass (4891 metres) to reach Leh (Laddakh) from Kulu. In 1947, when Kargil was attacked by Pakistan, Indian forces, arms and ammunition were sent to Laddakh by the Indian Union through this pass.
4. *Nanga Parbat Range:* This range spreads in Gilgit. Its height is 8107.68 metres above sea level and is utterly

devoid of vegetation. It was conquered by the Italian mountaineers in 1954. This is now under the unlawful possession of Pakistan.

5. *Harmukh Mountain:* This is a range of the Himalayas and is situated at a height of 5141.3 metres above sea level towards Bandipore between the rivers Jhelum and Kishan Ganga valley.
6. *Burzil Mountain:* It bifurcates Kashmir and Laddakh on which Burzil pass is situated at a height of 3200 metres above sea level.
7. *Amarnath Mountain:* This is famous for its holy Amarnath Cave, at a height of 5372 metresabove sea level, which thousands of pilgrims visit every year on Rakshabandan. They have to pass Mahagunas pass (1475 metres) on their way to Shri Amarnathji. Gwasharan (5450 metres) is situated in the Lidar valley towards Pahalgam; on it lies the famous glacier Kolahi. Sheeshnag Mountain also spreads in this valley. It is called Sheshnag as its peaks resemble the heads of seven big snakes.
8. *Toshmaidan:* Toshmaindan (4270 metres) and Kajinag (3700 metres) mountains lie in the Inner Himalayas. They remain clad with snow throughout the year, but during summer when the snow melts, the water flows down into the Jhelum river.
9. *Afarwat:* This mountain spreads through the Gulmarg valley. The famous spring Alpathar lies on its peak, from which Nullah Nagal comes out and flows down into the Wullar Lake.
10. *Pir Panjal Range:* It separates Kashmir valley from the outer Himalayas and is about 2621 Kms. in length and 50 Kms. in breadth. Famous Banihal pass (2832 metres) lies in the shape of a tunnel on its peak; it remains covered with snow during winter making it impassable. Now at a height of 2200 metres above sea level a new tunnel 'Jawahar Tunnel' has been constructed. The tunnel is 2825 metres long and it was opened for traffic on 22nd

Dec. 1956. On the other end of this range lie Baramula pass (1582 metres) and Hajipir pass (2750 metres). Hajipir joins Poonch and Uri. During 1965 Indo-Pak war, the Indian army had occupied this pass. Later on it was handed over to Pakistan.

11. *Shiwalik Range:* These hills extend from the north of the outer plains to middle mountains of the State reaching heights varying from 600 metres to 1500 metres above sea level.

12. *Volcanic mountains:* One volcanic peak, 'Soyamji' (1860 metres) is situated in North Machhipura (Handwara) and the other 'Kharewa' peak lies in Tehsil Pehalgam, which is dead so far; the former, however, continued eruption of lava for about 13 months during 1934.

    There is a temple on this peak and many sulphur springs are found at the foot of the hill. These volcanic mountains are the cause of earthquakes in Kashmir. So far twelve devastating earthquakes have occurred in Kashmir. Of these the earthquake of 1885 was the most devastating. Hundreds of houses collapsed, thousands of people died and there were cracks in the earth as a result of this earthquake.

Rivers, Lakes, Springs, Tributaries and Glaciers

Jammu and Kashmir State is well known for its charming scenery. There are beautiful springs, lakes, rivers and their tributaries. All these add to its scenic beauty. The Jhelum (Vyeth in Kashmiri, Vetesta in Sanskrit and Hydaspes in Greek) is the main waterway of the valley of Kashmir. It rises from a beautiful spring called Verinag. This spring is situated at the foot of a spur of the Pir Panjal mountain.

The Jhelum flows to a distance of 25.6 Kms to Khanabal like a nullah. From that place a number of tributaries join the Jhelum and make it navigable from Khannabal to WullarLake. Its total length in the valley is 177 kms. It flows in loops through the valley till it enters the Wullar; it flows out from its other side to Baramulla and then it enters the boundary of Pakistan. This part is not navigable, as the river makes a very deep bed and acquires a swift flow.

Srinagar town is situated on the either side of the river Jhelum. This enhances the beauty of the town making it a source of attraction for the tourists who stay in house-boats staying permanently in water on the banks of the river.

Tributaries of the River Jhelum

1. The Vishav is fed by the Kaunsarnag Lake which is about 3 Kms long. It joins the Jhelum below Bijbehara. Kounsarnag is at an elevation of about 4000 metres above sea level in the Panjal mountains to the south of Kashmir. Ice is present in the lake even in summer.

   The Vishav irrigates the Kulgam Tehsil and logs of timber cut in the forests in its upper course are floated down it to be transported to the valley.
2. The Romushi is another tributary of the Jhelum. It flows from Kharmarg to Pakharpur and flowing towards northeast. It joins the Jhelum at 75 deg. East longitude.
3. The Dudhganga is another tributary of the Jhelum that flows from Ludurmarg and rises in the central Pir Panjal near Tata Kuti mountain. Two mountain streams, the Sangesafed and the Yachera, form this river. This river flows through Batmalu Swamp near Srinagar.
4. The Sukhang is another important tributary. It rises near Gulmarg and irrigates a large area.
5. The Lidar is one of the largest tributaries of the Jhelum. It flows in a swift narrow stream from Sheeshnag lake to the east of Pahalgam. The Lidar passes through many villages of which Mattan (Martand) is very famous. The Kolahai and Sheeshnag streamlets join the Lidar at Pahalgam to make it a river.
6. The Ferozpore Nullah is an important water-way in the western mountains of Baramulla-Gulmarg area. It collects water from many mountain streams, small lakes and

springs. This mountaineous area is mostly full of snow even in summer.

7. The Sindh Nullah has its source in the Inner Himalayas at Dras and after it is fed by the Gangabal lake lying at Harmukh mountain (5150 meters), it joins the Jhelum at Shadipur. It is 96 Kms in length. The famous health resorts of Sonamarg and Ganderbal are situated on its banks. Its water is used for irrigation purposes and the 'Sindh Valley Hydroelectric Power Project' uses its water at Gandarbal to produce electric power. It is navigable from Gandarbal downwards.
8. The Flood Spill Channel was constructed in 1904 to relieve the strain on the Jhelum in the city of Srinagar. By taking 2/3rd of the total flow in the river it helps the river Jhelum to regulate its water level while passing through the city of Srinagar. The Jhelum rises during floods and the Channel saves the city from being flooded.

Lakes

1. The Wullar Lake in Kashmir is the largest fresh water lake in India. It is about 16 Kms. long and 9. 6 Kms wide with ill-defined shores. This lake lies between Bandipore and Sopore at a distance of 75 Kms. from Srinagar. The Jhelum enters this lake from the southeast and leaves it from the west. Storms rise in the lake everyday in the afternoon. The deepest part of the lake is at Watlab towards the hill called Baba Sukhuruddin in the northwest. Many small streams, Harbuji, Aarah, Erin and Pohru join this lake.
2. The Dal Lake is a beautiful lake near Srinagar. It is 8 Kms long and 6.4 Kms. wide. It is the flood-lung of the Jhelum. The famous Mughal gardens are situated around it. The lake is an ideal place for swimming and sailing in Shikaras and motorboats. Floating gardens are found in this lake where a large variety of vegetables is grown. The Dal Lake has two parts, the small Dal and the big Dal, separated by a swampy bund. The road round the

lake is called Boulevard. There are two artificial islands in the lake, Rupalank and Sonalank, built by Mughal Emperors. Nehru Park is the western terminus of the lake. The lake is a spot of great attraction for visitors, who enjoy staying in house-boats in the lake.

3. The Anchar Lake is a swampy area. The Sindh Nullah enters this lake from one side and flows out from the other. It is about 8 Kms long and 3 Kms. wide. Gandarbal is a famous township on its northwest bank.
4. The Mansbal Lake is at a distance of 29 Kms. from Srinagar and is situated at Safapore (Tehsil Gandarbal). It is 5 Kms long and one Km. wide. It is connected with the Jhelum by a canal near Sumbal. Mughal Emperors have built a summer palace on its bank.
5. The Harvan Lake is situated at a distance of 21 Kms from Srinagar. It is 278 meters long, 137 meters wide and 18 metres deep. This lake is a source of water supply to Srinagar city.
6. The Hokarsar Lake lies on Baramulla road about 13 Kms. from Srinagar. It is about 5 Kms. long and 1.5 Kms. wide. Willow trees are grown in abundance around its banks.
7. The Konsarnag or Vishno Pad Lake is situated in the Pir Panjal range at a height of 4000 meters above sea level to the south of Shopian. It is about 5 Kms. long and 3 Kms. wide and is the source of the river Vishav. It is at a distance of 34 Kms. from Shopian.
8. The Gangabal Lake is situated at a height of 3570.4M. on the peak of Harmukh mountain. Hindus consider it a sacred lake.
9. The Sheshnag Lake is situated near Vavjan, enroute to Shri Amarnath cave. It is at a distance of 28 Kms. from Pahalgam.
10. The Neelang Lake is situated in Tehsil Badgam at a distance of 10 Kms from Nagam. It is a beautiful lake with dense forests around it.

11. There are two more lakes, Tarsar and Marsar that lie on the northern slope of the Harmukh mountain. Marsar lake is the origin of the Canal Sharab Kohl that provides water to the fountains that play in the Mughal Gardens. Marsar Lake flows into the Lidar which is one of the largest tributaries of the Jhelum.
12. Sokh and Dokh are two frozen lakes situated at Harmukh Mountain. These are said to be two tear drops of Parvati; one a warm tear drop indicating happiness and other a cold one showing grief.

Springs

Kashmir valley abounds in numerous springs of which Verinag (source of the Jhelum), Martand (Anantnag), Achhabal (Anantnag), Kukarnag (Anantnag), Chashma Shahi (famous for its fresh and digestive water, situated near Srinagar on one side of the Boulevard road), Tullamulla or Khirbhawani (a sacred spring), Vicharnag, Sukhnag, Vishnosar and Harmukat Ganga in Srinagar area and Chirnagand Vasaknag in Anantnag are very famous.

GEOGRAPHY AND CLIMATE

Jammu and Kashmir is home to several valleys such as the Kashmir Valley, Tawi Valley, Chenab Valley, Poonch Valley, Sind Valley and Lidder Valley. The main Kashmir Valley is 100 km (62 mi) wide and 15,520.3 km (5,992.4 sq mi) in area. The Himalayas divide the Kashmir valley from Ladakh while the Pir Panjal range, which encloses the valley from the west and the south, separates it from the Great Plains of northern India. Along the northeastern flank of the Valley runs the main range of the Himalayas. This densely settled and beautiful valley has an average height of 1,850 metres (6,070 ft) above sea-level but the surrounding Pir Panjal range has an average elevation of 5,000 metres (16,000 ft).

Because of Jammu and Kashmir's wide range of elevations, its biogeography is diverse. Northwestern thorn scrub forests

and Himalayan subtropical pine forests are found in the low elevations of the far southwest. These give way to a broad band of western Himalayan broadleaf forests running from northwest-southeast across the Kashmir Valley. Rising into the mountains, the broadleaf forests grade into western Himalayan subalpine conifer forests. Above the tree line are found northwestern Himalayan alpine shrub and meadows. Much of the northeast of the state is covered by the Karakoram-West Tibetan Plateau alpine steppe. Around the highest elevations, there is no vegetation, simply rock and ice.

Srinagar- Yatra- Hindu holy cave

Division	Area km²	Percentage Area
Kashmir	15,948	15.73%
Jammu	26,293	25.93%
Ladakh	59,146	58.33%
India-administrated Jammu and Kashmir	101,387 km²	100%

The Jhelum River is the only major Himalayan river which flows through the Kashmir valley. The Indus, Tawi, Ravi and Chenab are the major rivers flowing through the state. Jammu and Kashmir is home to several Himalayan glaciers. With an average altitude of 5,753 metres (18,875 ft) above sea-level, the Siachen Glacier is 76 km (47 mi) long making it the longest Himalayan glacier.

The climate of Jammu and Kashmir varies greatly owing to its rugged topography. In the south around Jammu, the climate is typically monsoonal, though the region is sufficiently far west to average 40 to 50 mm (1.6 to 2 inches) of rain per month between January and March. In the hot season, Jammu city is very hot and can reach up to 40 °C (104 °F) whilst in July and August, very heavy though erratic rainfall occurs with monthly extremes of up to 650 millimeters (25.5 inches). In September, rainfall declines, and by October conditions are hot but extremely dry, with minimal rainfall and temperatures of around 29 °C (84 °F).

Indus River near Leh

Across from the Pir Panjal range, the South Asian monsoon is no longer a factor and most precipitation falls in the spring from southwest cloudbands. Because of its closeness to the Arabian Sea, Srinagar receives as much as 635 millimetres (25 in) of rain from this source, with the wettest months being March to May with around 85 millimetres (3.3 inches) per month. Across from the main Himalaya Range, even the southwest cloudbands break up and the climate of Ladakh and Zanskar is extremely dry and cold. Annual precipitation is only

around 100 mm (4 inches) per year and humidity is very low. In this region, almost all above 3,000 metres (9,750 ft) above sea level, winters are extremely cold. In Zanskar, the average January temperature is "20 °C ("4 °F) with extremes as low as "40 °C ("40 °F). All the rivers freeze over and locals make river crossings during this period because their high levels from glacier melt in summer inhibits crossing. In summer in Ladakh and Zanskar, days are typically a warm 20 °C (68 °F), but with the low humidity and thin air nights can still be cold.

Topographic map of J&K (Kashmir valley, Jammu region and Ladakh region are visible by altitude)

Mountains in Jammu and Kashmir

JAMMU PROVINCE

The strip of level land at the northernmost extremity of the plains of the Punjab which touches the low ridges of the hills and spreads over a large tract, constitutes what is called the "region of the outer hills." Varying in height from 60 m to 1,200 m above the sea level, these rugged hills run parallel to one another enclosing small, narrow valleys.

The province of Jammu lies between the "outer hills" region bounding the valley of Kashmir in the south, and the hilly tract extending to the plains of the Punjab. The river Ravi flows in the east of this region and the river Jhelum in the west. The river Chenab issues forth from the mountain into the plains near the town of Akhnur and flows through the Jammu district before entering the plains of the Punjab.

The "outer hills" region consists of Kdhampur, Ramnagar, and Rampur. The rugged hills give way in the north and northeast to the outer hills of the Shivaliks, 1,200 m to 3,600 m above the sea level. There is a continuous rise in elevation to what are conveniently called the "middle hills" or the middle Himalayas. In this region lie the districts of Batote, Bhadarwah, Kishtwar, Doda, and Ramban.

Jammu city, the winter capital of the state, stands on the spurs of a rugged hill overlooking the plains and the river Tawi. The city is about 300 m above the sea level and about 4 km. wide. According to 1991 census, the city had a population of 1,207,996. The prominent features of the city are its temples, whose pointed spires can be seen from afar. Other towns in this plain, and to the east of the river Chenab are Basoli, Ramkot, Ramnagar, and Samba and to the west of Chenab, Akhnur and Bhimber.

The Jammu district occupies an area of 26,089.4 sq. km. The relief features of the province provide interesting climatic as well as floral phenomena. There is a sort of wind divide starting from Poonch and extending to the southern edge of the Pir Panjal. The area has summer precipitation. As in the plains, the southwest monsoons cause rain in the "outer plains" area and the "outer hills" region. As the altitude rises towards the "middle mountains" area of Batote, Bhadarwah, Kishtwar, Padar, and Banihal, the summer rainfall averages 45 inches (113 cm). Riasi and Poonch get more than 60 inches (150 cm) of rainfall annually. The "outer plains" areas of Ramnagar, Ramkot, Samba, Basoli, Akhnur, and Bhimber experience the extremes of tropical heat. The average annual rainfall in Jammu district is nearly 45 inches (113 cm). The hot season lasts from April to June, followed by the rainy season from July to September. Winter lasts from October to March.

There is a luxurious growth of vegetation all over the "outer hill" and the "middle mountains" areas which is mostly of tropical variety. The upper reaches of the mountains are thickly covered with coniferous forests. The lower regions have forests of silver fir, deodar, spruce, oak, and pine. The best varieties of pine and deodar are found in the dense forests of Kishtwar and Bhadarwah. The "plain area" bounds in cactus varieties of bushes and trees.

The main crops in the Jammu valley are maize, rice, millet, barley, and wheat. Jammu province is rich in minerals coal, bauxite, copper, zinc, and lead are abundant. Sapphire mines are located at higher elevations in the Papar valley. Semi - precious stones like beryl and aquamarine and crystals like quartz and felopar are also found in the region. Riasi has coal, gem stones, gypsum, clay, copper, bauxite, and iron ore.

Though little known, the tableland of Kishtwar is flanked by the high and steep mountains of the "middle mountains" region, the highest point being 4,089 km. above sea level. It has an area of 7,311 sq. km. Kistwar is famous for mines of sapphire and rubies. The climate is pleasant and bracing in summer and cold in winter.

Kishtwar and Bhadarwah, with heavily forested mountains are regular haunts of hunters. They can hunt panthers, black and red bear, wild goat, ibex, musk deer, wolf, barasingha, pig, Himalayan chamois, leopard, etc. In the river beds, swamps and low forests, a variety of winged game-duck, goose, chakor, monal pheasant, partridge and snipe are found in preserves for sportsmen.

Saffron is grown here. Black cumin, medicinal herbs like banafsha, kahzaban, dhoop, musk, bala, artemesia and belladonna are grown in the region. Narcotic herbs are also found. Blankets and leather goods of the region are famous.

KASHMIR VALLEY

The valley of Kashmir is a unique, oval plain, approximately 134 km. in length and 32 to 40 km. in breadth, with an average height of 1,800 m above the sea level, and nested securely among the Pir Panjal range of the Himalayas.

The mountains which surround the valley are varied in form, height, and colour. To the east stands hoary-headed Harmukh (5,150 m), the formidable mountain guarding the valley of the Sindh. Further south is Mahadev and the lofty ranges of Gwasha Brari (5,425 m). The peak of Amarnath (5,280 m) also lies in this area. On the southwest is the Pir Panjal range with peaks 4,500 m high and to the north are ranges of the Karakorams and the Himalayas. Himalayas is dominated by the majestic Nanga Parbat (7,980 m), also called by the poetic name of Diyamir. Covered with snow all the year round and rising glistening white, Nanga Parbat is the fifth highest mountain in the world. Latitude wise, Kashmir corresponds to Damascus in Syria, Fez in Morocco, and South Carolina in the United States.

The legend that the Kashmir valley was a vast lake, Satisar, in pre-historical times, corresponds with the results of geological observations. The sandstone rock at the western corner of the basin was most probably formed by volcanic action. The lake was drained by the deepening of the Baramulla gorge - the result of the slow process of erosion spread over geological years. Tradition has it that the drainer of the lake was Kashyap, after whom the valley was called Kashyap-mar, which, with the passage of time, became Kashmir. According to an interpretation, Kashmir is a prakrit compound with its components Kas meaning "a channel" and Mir, "a mountain" - the compound word adding to a "a rock trough." In the Puranas, Kashmir is called gerek (hill) because of its overwhelming hilly features. The word Kashmir has been shortened by Kashmiris into Kashmir. Kashmiris call their language Koshur or Kashur.

The shape of the valley is that of an elliptical saucer. The floor of the vast valley is built of small consolidated lake beds and alluvial soils. Numerous plateaus, locally known as Karewas, stand up isolated in the middle of the valley.

Anantnag is another ancient town of Kashmir, about 64 km. to the north of Srinagar. It is an exotic town full of springs and streams run in every other compound. Some of these are sulphurous springs, which have curative qualities.

Other major towns are Baramulla and Sopore; both situated on the Jhelum after the river enters the Wular Lake and emerges from it.

LADDAKH

Beyond the valley of Kashmir, the inner Himalayas rising in the north and east contain the frontier region of the state. The territory comprises the three geographical divisions of Laddakh, Baltistan, and Dardistan. Out of the total area of the state of 138,992.1 sq. km, the district of Laddakh (97,782 sq. km) covers 70.4% of the total area.

The province of Laddakh touches the Chinese border on the north, merges into Tibet in the east and is contained along the south by the extension of the great Himalayan range. The Karakoram Range of mountain lies in the north Laddakh. The second highest peak in the world, K2 (Mt.Godwin 8611 metres) crowns one of its many tall mountains. The Karakoram pass (5,517.64 m) is situated towards the northeast of Karakoram, in an area where China, Tibet, and Laddakh meet. This pass facilitates a direct route from India to China.

Until some years ago, Laddakh used to be the gateway to Tibet, connecting India with Tibet and east Turkistan. As such, it was an important trade centre, also being the meeting point of the Tibetan, Indian, Chinese, and Islamic cultures and traditions.

Leh, the headquarter of Laddakh (3,521 m above the sea level) is a fascinating town built on a hillside and surrounded by rocky hills. It was once the commercial nerve centre of Central Asia just as Hong Kong is of the Far East. Traders thronged Leh from Turkey, Arab countries, Iran, and Afghanistan. Leh town is full of orchards, groves, gardens and monasteries and is crowded with people. Poplars and Willows are aplenty. Apples, apricots and giant-size melons are grown in these orchards.

Laddakh is a mountainous terrain between the Himalayas

and the Kuenlum mountains. One of the highest habitations in the world, Laddakh has an elevation ranging between 2,400 m and 4,500 m above the sea level. The average height of its mountain is between 5000 and 7000 m. Its valleys, about 500 sq. km. in area, lie along the headwaters of the Indus, the Sutlej, and the Chenab rivers. The Indus, having originated hundreds of kilometres further east from near the Kailash Mountain and the Mansarovar Lake in Tibet, flows in an almost straight line from northwest to the southeast of Laddakh. The river enters the region of Skardu in Baltistan.

An interesting spectacle in Laddakh is represented by hot springs and geysers roaring and throwing steaming hot water up to a height of 150 m and projecting fantastic rainbow colours. These fountains of water represent phenomenon in winter when the boiling water comes down in the shape of ice blocks with the impact of chilly winds and form mounds next to the geysers.

In the northeast of Leh, at the town of Nyoma, lies an unusual terrain, where the colour of the soil and rocks is purple. The awe-inspiring mountain peaks seem to touch the sky. There is a conspicuous absence of life of any form and hence it has been aptly called the "Land of the broken moon", a truly poetical name.

Over the Laddakh range and in the north of Leh is the road to Khardung La (5,600 m above the sea level), the highest road in the world - a veritable walk over thick ice-sheets, ice-walls, and glaciers with the Karakoram range in the background. Further on, Chushul, the Pangong salt water lake, is about 112 km. long. Its water is blue-green and sometimes indigo-purple.

Kargil (about 2,750 m above the sea level) has a similar network of mountains around it. The people of Kargil do some farming and raise sheep. Their houses are built of stone and plastered with thick layers of mud to escape the extreme rigours of the cold. They profess Islam.

The high altitude of Laddakh and Kargil and high mountains encircling the region give it a unique climate- absolute dryness (the annual rainfall is about 4 inches, *i.e.* 10 cm, and there is very little snow), arctic cold and extremes of weather. It is burning hot by day and piercing cold by night, very hot in summer, and extremely cold in winter.

FLORA AND FAUNA OF JAMMU AND KASHMIR

Jammu & Kashmir is a mystifying land. It is a picturesque collage of various elements of nature that makes it an ideal tourist destination. The northern frontier of the state is fortified with the majestic mountains of the Himalaya Range. These ranges and their snow capped peaks complete a picturesque landscape that includes crystal clear streams and lush green vegetation.

Jammu and Kashmir is not a homogeneous land. It is marked by undulating topography and varied soil types that lead to the growth of diverse plants. These in turn, support numerous life forms to constitute an ecological pyramid.

In terms of climate, Jammu and Kashmir is unique. The vast distribution of topographical features is a cause of this fact. The controlling factor of the climate is the Himalayas. Except the dry plateaus of Ladakh, the state receives ample amounts of rainfall. The land is crisscrossed by perennial streams of fresh water. The streams water the land and sustain the lives of the people that inhabit the land. Winter season sees extensive precipitation in terms of snowfall. In the winter, the snow resembles a vast sheet of white blanket covering the valleys.

Culture and human settlements have also been altered by the pattern of the climatic variations of the region. Three socio-cultural regions have been established in the state. Each region has a set of distinct cultural patterns that coexist in harmony under the umbrella of Jammu and Kashmir. The Easternmost region of Ladakh is the stronghold of predominantly Tibetan culture. The southern state is the foothills of the Himalayas that are the home of tribes such as the Dogras that migrated centuries ago. The northernmost region outlines the beautiful valley of Kashmir and its majestic beauty. Each of these regions contributes heavily to make Jammu and Kashmir an epitome of cross-cultural harmony.

The scenic beauty of Jammu and Kashmir is enchanting, to say the least. The combination of nature, heritage and history make the state an enchanting land. Among many other traits that distinguish the land of Jammu & Kashmir, the flora and fauna of the state is one of prime importance. It is home to a bewildering variety of animals that inhabit the mountainous terrain. The flora that grow on the rich soil supports the variety of fauna found in the area. The flora has a defining impact on the lives of the people as well and is extremely beneficial for maintaining their cultural heritage.

The flora of Jammu and Kashmir includes broad-leaved trees as well as conifers. Shrubs and herbs of immense anthropogenic importance sprout in the fertile reaches of the valleys. Trees such as rhododendron constitute the thick forests high in the hills. The floral type varies with variation of the elevation. The forests are inhabited by organisms from every member of the animal family. Mammals such as leopards and bears are found in numbers in the state. Even the barren land of Ladakh has a distinct set of animals equipped to thrive in the cold inhospitable zones. Besides, birds, amphibians, reptiles and insects form an intrinsic part of the landscape that has no parallels on earth.

The Flora

Describing the flora of Jammu and Kashmir is like trying to catalogue a library that has an extensive collection of books. Many of the species have not even been documented properly. Nevertheless, it should suffice to say that the state possess a rich diversity of flora. An estimate puts the total number of plant species in the state at over 3000. These are unevenly distributed throughout the three regions of the state. For example, the dry frontiers of Ladakh have about 880 species, most of them able to withstand extreme climatic conditions. In

Jammu, the number is over 500 species of plants. These estimations are inadequate since they include only certain groups of plants. The inventory is inadequate in the strictest sense and is continuously being updated to include lesser studied forms.

The flora of the state have a high degree of endemism. Some of the families of plants that are found here are found nowhere else. The plants that are found in Jammu and Kashmir are a majorly important part of the people that inhabit the state. The forests are the source of fodder, food, honey and other such commodities that lend a lot to the identity of the locals. Several plants with medicinal properties have been identified in the region. Many of these plants are used by locals as rudimentary medicines. The forests cover over 20% of the geographical area of the state constituting a vast reserve of natural wealth.

Phyto Geography and Vegetation Types

Throughout the geological history, the region has seen an evolutionary sequence of plants forms colonizing and thriving under different sets of conditions. The continuous influence of the climate and geomorphologic features on the flora and fauna of the state persists to this day.

Jammu and Kashmir has three distinct regions of floral pattern:

Alpine Desert Vegetation of Ladakh

Ladakh is a cold desert and extreme conditions are prevalent throughout the year. The plant groups that have successfully survived the barren landscape are evolved to minimize water loss. Typically, they grow in the vicinity of moist stream channels.

Temperate vegetation of Kashmir: The foothills of the Karakoram ranges were once covered with a luxuriant canopy of thick forests occupying the valleys and plains. Unfortunately, human settlements have wiped out many stretches of forests for cultivation of food crops. Still, the few remaining patches of forests give us a glimpse of the richness the state possesses. The valleys are marked by swampy, linear patches of forests delineated on the south by the Pir Panjal range.

Subtropical Vegetation of Jammu

Jammu is situated at a much lower elevation than the rest of Jammu and Kashmir. At this altitude, the climate supports dry and deciduous forests. The monsoon season witnesses widespread inundation of the low lying areas that become breeding grounds for numerous aquatic plants.

Aquatic Vegetation

The rugged mountainous terrain of the Pir Panjal range is situated at altitudes above 4000 meters. At such an elevation, the lakes of the Kashmir valley do not have appropriate conditions to sustain major plant life. Below the snow line, the lakes are teeming with aquatic life. These lakes show zonation which is a regular feature. The core of such water bodies harbour plants that are submerged under the water. Only some parts of the plant, such as the flowers or the fruits float above the surface. The buffer or intermediate floral varieties are found in the shallower parts that have floating leaves. The outermost zone of plants is found along the fringes of the lakes with the majority of the plant body standing above the water level. Some free floating varieties are found here, as well.

Many lakes in Kashmir have floating islands that are artificially created and used for cultivation of crops.

Threatened Plants

The rich flora of Jammu and Kashmir has been subjected to degradation, and many of the species stands on the brink of extinction. The reasons for this are a subject of intense debate.

The extinction of species can be ascribed to two controlling factors; those that are controlled by natural processes and those created by human activities. In the past, natural processes led to the decline of countless species, culminating in major extinction events. The evolution of the earth has seen numerous extinction events. These events have their cause root in various climatic factors and changes in the atmosphere of the earth. In the past, the various extinction events occurred over a long time, allowing other species to colonize and substitute their place.

The current rates of extinction are alarming because of its sheer magnitude and speed. Throughout the globe, the natural world has been mutilated and destroyed to enable human requirements to be fulfilled. The burgeoning growth of the population has put immense pressure on land resources and forests. The destruction of forests has a cascading effect, which in due course of time threatens entire ecosystems and the population which depend on it.

Jammu and Kashmir's floral collection are important for sustaining the culture and traditional continuity of the people. Many of the plants found here have medicinal value, a property that has increased relevance in our combat against deadly diseases. Jammu and Kashmir is an important portion of India's biodiversity. The areas of Kashmir, and the slopes of the Himalaya have been identified as a 'biodiversity hotspot', among 26 such identified localities in India. The increasing rate of deforestation has destabilized the foothills

The Fauna

Jammu and Kashmir is divided into three different parts namely Jammu, Kashmir Valley and Ladakh. Each of these regions has separate sets of fauna in response to the different conditions prevalent in each of the regions. The state boasts of an impressive 16% of the total faunal species in India. Birds are the primary contributor to this high diversity of chordate species. Apart from birds, the state has a high diversity of many other forms of organisms such as mammals and reptiles, and lesser-known animals such as fishes, amphibians and an infinite number of insects. The state is strategically positioned at the confluence of major climatic zones that account for the high diversity. This factor lends high endemic character to the organisms that are found in the state.

The diversity of avian species is remarkable. The 358 species of birds that have been recorded in the state can be catalogued into 179 genera and 16 orders. Many of these birds are migratory and navigate treacherous journeys to reach the promising land. The waters of the state provide habitat for 44 species of fish, categorized into 14 genera. Amphibians, such as frogs have been placed under 14 genera. The insect collection is infinite, with many of the species yet to be discovered.

Mammals are represented by 75 species. These species themselves are subdivided into subspecies, represented by 54 genera further classified into 21 families. Among the mammals, it is the carnivores that occupy a chunk of the total mammals.

The abundance of faunal riches Jammu and Kashmir possess is enviable. The state is the last refuge for many threatened animals and the state is doing the needful to prolong their survival.

The protected areas of the region, its national parks and wildlife sanctuaries have been established. These provide a safe haven for these species for visitors to see and appreciate the rich natural heritage the state possess.

Dachigam National Park

Dachigam National Park is located just 20 kilometers from the state capital Srinagar. It houses a broad range of flora due to the great differences in the elevation. The high relief feature of the park forms the core of the high diversity in the distribution pattern of the organisms. The high relief is able to accommodate various types of vegetations from conifers to broad-leaved forests. The park presents scenic views of the disturbed natural landscape. The 141 square kilometers has been planned to incorporate surrounding areas into its perimeter. The forest is the natural habitat of one the famous Kashmiri stag or Hangul. Besides, other animals such as musk deer, leopards, snow leopards and Himalayan bears can be found in this preserve. Numerous species of birds such as the Monal, Sparrows and Bulbuls can be spotted in this serene surrounding. Dachigam National Park has remarkable accommodation facilities. It even has a guest house inside the limits of the park to provide for a wild holiday experience. The spring season is ideal for a visit to the park.

Ramnagar Wildlife Sanctuary

Ramnagar Wildlife Sanctuary is situated on the outskirts of Jammu town. The elevation of the wildlife sanctuary varies between 400 to 600 meters. The reserve is known for its species of deer such as the Nilgai and other mammals. Being close to Jammu town, it is a favorite getaway for tourists visiting the area. In terms of area, Ramnagar Wildlife Sanctuary occupies 31 square kilometers. However, the small size can be deceptive while considering the immense interests it possesses for wildlife enthusiasts.

Gulmarg Biosphere

Throughout the world, Gulmarg Biosphere reserve is known for its population of the musk deer. The nature reserve consists of almost 180 square kilometers of a mixed variety of forests providing refuge for some of the rarest species. The vegetation found here is of alpine type with conifers being the dominating plant type. Besides, shrubs and herbs such as Heterantha cover much of the forest floor. Apart from the musk deer, the animal population in Gulmarg is represented by Hangul and bears, along with jungle cats and leopards. The park has two varieties of bears, the brown bear and the black bear. The park boasts of bird species such as the Monal and the Griffon vulture. The ideal time for visiting the park is winter.

KASHMIR FLORA & FAUNA

Kashmir is rich in the cultural diversity of the people, as well as diversity of flora and fauna in the forest areas, and domesticated species outside the forest. Plant diversity is the life support of almost all terrestrial eco-systems, with both humans and animals being entirely dependent on plants directly or indirectly.

The state of Jammu and Kashmir has a fairly rich diversity of plant life, and on this the people depend for their daily needs of food, medicine, fuel, fiber, etc. The varied plant life also contributes to the food and habitat needs of the wild and domesticated animals in the state. Plants are also an integral part of the social fabric of the state. The environmental, social and economic values of plants are very well known. On the other hand, the faunal component of the bio-diversity of the state is rich, with interesting and unique forms both in the forest zones and above the forest-line. The variety of animal forms ranges from higher groups like vertebrates, including mammals, birds, reptiles, amphibians, and lower groups like invertebrates including insects and even unicellular micro-organisms.

The flora

The flora of Himalayan Kashmir comprises about 3,054 species. About 880 species are found in Ladakh. The flora of the Jammu district comprises 506 species. These figures include only the angiosperms, gymnosperms and pteridophytes. The species lists of different districts are being continually updated in taxonomic publications. The lower plants like fungi and algae have not been studied exhaustively; information on the micro-flora of isolated regions is available for some plant orders and families only. The plants of the western Himalayas are well known for their medicinal properties.

This area is a storehouse of medicinal and aromatic plants, which are used in pharmaceutical and perfume industries. The list includes 55 species of important medicinal and aromatic plants. There are 11 medicinal plants in the temperate, cold, arid regions of Jammu and Kashmir. Several medicinal plants grow wild in the temperate and alpine habitats. Some native medicinal plants have been taken up for cultivation, e.g. Dioscorea deltoidea is now cultivated for its tubers which are rich in diosgenin and yield cortisone, a steroid hormone.

Chinar

Locally called "The Booune" in the Kashmiri language, Chinar tree holds a special place in Kashmiri civilization. Almost every village in the valley has a Chinar tree. You can experience a cool breeze under the shadow of this majestic tree which is very conducive to health.

It is unfortunate that in recent years the number of Chinar trees is decreasing. It is no wonder that if the present trend continues, the day is not far-off when the tree will see its extinction from the land of Kashmir. However, it is heartening to note the government is making its honest best to stop the illegal felling of this great tree of Kashmir.

Chinar is a gigantic sized tree, found growing throughout valley. Its scientific name is platanus orientalis. Its family is plataneae. A deciduous tree, Chinar traces its origin to Greece. Its incredible beauty has to be seen to be believed. The tree is at its most elegance and exuberance during autumn. Though its majesty can be seen all through the year. Iqbal, the poet of the East, traces the warmth of the Kashmir soil to the "blaze of Chinars it nurses in its bosom".

Chinar grows up to a height of 25 meters and a girth exceeding 50 feet in certain cases. This tree with the largest circumference of 60 feet is located at a village named Chattergam in central Kashmir.

These days conscious efforts are being made to undertake plantation of this tree to other states. The tree has been successfully planted in New Delhi, Chandigarh, Dehradun and Meerut. But the size and girth attained in these places are no parallel to those of the tree in Kashmir valley.

Fauna

The fauna of Jammu and Kashmir is diverse due to its unique location and climatic condition. About 16% of the Indian mammals, birds, reptiles, amphibians and butterflies are presented in the state. Birds contribute much to the chordate diversity following by mammals, reptiles, fishes and amphibians. The state is home to about 75 species of mammals, besides several sub-species, belonging to 54 genera, 21 families and 8 orders. Carnivores represent 32% of the total mammalian fauna in the state. Of the 19 species of the ungulates reported from the state, 13 have been listed as globally threatened.

The avian diversity of the state varies seasonally and available data suggests the existence of as many as 358 species of birds belonging to 179 genera, 51 families under 16 orders. The state is home to 14 species of amphibians belonging to 6 genera, 5 families and 1 order, and 68 species of reptiles belonging to 43 genera, 12 families and 2 orders. The available data suggests that 44 species of fishes belonging to 14 genera under 5 families occur in the state. The available data also reveals that as many as 225 species of insects, besides several sub-species, belonging to 136 genera, 35 families and 4 orders occur in the state.

Jammu and Kashmir is home to number of species that are listed as endangered like the Kashmiri stag called 'Hangul' and snow leopard that has survived here from times unknown. You can see many more fascinating and exquisite forms of life in the many national parks and sanctuaries that are here in the state.

Dachigam National Park

Dachigam National Park is situated around 22 km away from Srinagar and covers an area of more than 141-sq. km. Located amidst the mountains, there is a huge variation in the altitude of the park that ranges from 1600 m to 4200m above sea level. Due to this difference, the park is divided into two regions, the upper region and the lower region. The park is without a doubt the most scenic of all the parks in the state. The animal for which the park is most famous is the endangered species Hangul, the Kashmiri stag. Other animal species that you will see in the park are Musk deer, Brown Bear, Leopards, Jungle Cats and many more. The park is also home to numerous rare and splendid looking birds like Black Bulbuls, Cinnamon sparrows, Himalayan Monals and Kashmir Flycatcher. There is accommodation available inside the park as well.

Gulmarg Biosphere

This is a park that is rich in everything, right from flora and fauna to avi-fauna. Gulmarg Biosphere is located at a distance of 48 km from Srinagar and covers an area of 180 sq. km. The park has acquired fame because it has been able to protect most of the animals that are found here, which are Musk Deer, Hangul, Brown Bear, Leopard and Black Bear. Most of the park is covered in forest consisting mainly of Conifers. The common birds that you will see here are Griffon Vulture, Monal, Koklas, European Hoopoe and many more. Best time to come here is between September and March for mammals and March to May for birds.

6

Economy

INTRODUCTION

Economy of Jammu and Kashmir

Statistics

GDP	1.32 lakh crore (US$18 billion) (2016–17 est.)
GDP rank	21st
GDP growth	14% (2016–17 est.)
GDP by sector	Agriculture 22%
Industry	25%
Services	53% (2015)
Labour force by occupation	Agriculture 64%
Industry	11%
Services	25% (2015)
Public finances	
Public debt	49.25% of GDP (2016–17 est.)
Revenues	53,202 crore (US$7.4 billion) (2016–17 est.)
Expenses	64,669 crore (US$9.0 billion) (2016–17 est.)

All values, unless otherwise stated, are in US dollars.

Tourism forms an integral part of the state's economy. Shown here is the Shalimar Gardens. Mughal emperor Jahangir inscribed Amir Khusrau's famous *paradise on Earth* verse in the gardens.

Jammu and Kashmir's economy is predominantly dependent on agriculture and allied activities. The Kashmir Valley is known for its sericulture and cold-water fisheries. Wood from Kashmir is used to make high-quality cricket bats, popularly known as *Kashmir Willow*. Kashmiri saffron is very famous and brings the state a handsome amount of foreign exchange. Agricultural exports from Jammu and Kashmir include apples, barley, cherries, corn, millet, oranges, rice, peaches, pears, saffron, sorghum, vegetables, and wheat, while manufactured exports include handicrafts, rugs, and shawls.

Horticulture plays a vital role in the economic development of the state. With an annual turnover of over 3 billion(US$42 million), apart from foreign exchange of over 800 million (US$11 million), this sector is the next biggest source of income in the state's economy. The region of Kashmir is known for its horticulture industry and is the wealthiest region in the state. Horticultural produce from the state includes apples, apricots, cherries, pears, plums, almonds and walnuts.

The Doda district has deposits of high-grade sapphire. Though small, the manufacturing and services sector is growing rapidly, especially in the Jammu division. In recent years, several consumer goods companies have opened manufacturing units in the region.

The Associated Chambers of Commerce and Industry of India (ASSOCHAM) has identified several industrial sectors which can attract investment in the state, and accordingly, it is working with the union and the state government to set up industrial parks and special economic zones. In the fiscal year 2005–06, exports from the state amounted to 11.5 billion(US$160 million). However, industrial development in the state faces several major constraints including extreme mountainous landscape and power shortage. The Jammu & Kashmir Bank, which is listed as a S&P CNX 500conglomerate, is based in the state. It reported a net profit of 598 million (US$8.3 million) in 2008.

The Government of India has been keen to economically integrate Jammu and Kashmir with the rest of India. The state is one of the largest recipients of grants from New Delhi, totalling US$812 million per year. It has a mere 4% incidence of poverty, one of the lowest in the country.

In an attempt to improve the infrastructure in the state, Indian Railways is constructing the ambitious Jammu–Baramulla line project at a cost of more than US$2.5 billion. Trains run on the 130 km Baramula-Banihal section. The 17.5 km Qazigund-Banihal section through the 11 km long Pir Panjal Railway Tunnel was commissioned. Udhampur-Katra section of the track was commissioned early in July 2014. The Katra-Banihal section is under construction. The route crosses major earthquake zones and is subjected to extreme temperatures of cold and heat, as well as inhospitable terrain, making it an extremely challenging engineering project. It is expected to increase tourism and travel to Kashmir. Three other railway lines, the Bilaspur–Mandi–Leh railway, Srinagar-Kargil-Leh railway and the Jammu-Poonch railway have been proposed.

Year	State's Gross Domestic Product (in million INR)
1980	11,860
1985	22,560
1990	36,140

1995	80,970
2000	147,500
2006	539,850 million (US$7.5 billion)
2016	132,307 crore (US$18 billion)

AGRICULTURE

Given below is a table of 2015 national output share of select agricultural crops and allied segments in Jammu and Kashmir based on 2011 prices

Segment	National Share %
Walnut	94.1
Cherry	93.8
Almond	90.5
Apple	25.2
Pear	22.3
Wool and hair	10.1

AGRICULTURE IN JAMMU AND KASHMIR

The practice of cultivating the soil in order to produce crops and domestication of animals and pastoral farming are known as agriculture. The agricultural processes of a region are directly controlled by the prevailing physical environmental condition (temperature, precipitation, terrain, soil etc.) and the socio-cultural milieu (land tenancy, size of holding, technology, workforce, family requirements, irrigation, power, roads, marketing, aspirations of the growers, etc.).

The present article gives a concise account of the general land-use, cropping pattern, crops concentration, crops combinations and the agricultural operations being carried out in the different agro-climatic regions of the Jammu and Kashmir state.

Jammu and Kashmir is essentially a mountainous state in which only about 30 per cent of the reporting area is under cultivation. Agriculture is the mainstay of the people as it provides employment, directly or indirectly to about 70 per cent of the workforce.

It contributes about 65 per cent of the state revenue which explains the overdependence of the state on agriculture. Land is, however, limited and therefore, its judicious utilization is necessary to meet the growing need of the tremendously increasing population and for the sustainability of soils, ecosystems and environment.

Land Utilization

Land utilization statistics provide the area figures, showing the distribution of the total geographical area/reporting area of a region/country into vari-ous uses. Although detailed statistics of land use for the country, showing the area of land put to different uses, are continuously available since 1884, but in the case of Jammu and Kashmir there are several data gaps.

In India, in general, the land has been classified under different categories.

In 1890-91, a five-fold classification of the total geographical area of the country was made and the land was put under the categories of:

(i) Forest,

(ii) Area not available for cultivation,

(iii) Current fallow,

(iv) Net area sown.

In 1949-50, the land classification was, however, revised. The revised classification has been accepted for use by all the states of India, since 1950-51. The new classification has been introduced by all the states except West Bengal and Manipur where agricultural data is still recorded on the basis of old classification.

The existing classification of land use in the country is as follows:

1. Forest
2. Land not available for cultivation:

(a) Land put to non-agricultural uses, and

(b) Barren and uncultivated land.

3. Other uncultivated land excluding fallow lands:

(a) Permanent pastures and other grazing lands,

(b) Miscellaneous tree-crops and groves not included in the net area sown, and

(c) Cultivable waste.

4. Fallow land:

(a) Fallow land, other than current fallow, and

(b) Current fallow.

5. Net area sown.

General Land-use

The total geographical area of the state is 2.23 lakh sq km including those parts which are under the occupation of Pakistan and China. About 92 per cent of the geographical area of the state consists of high mountains rugged topography and only 5 per cent is available for culti-vation.

Being, hilly, mountainous and snow covered, it is only the gentle slopes (below 15°) which may be developed as orchards and pastures after heavy investment. The proportion of old fallow and current fallow is 0.29 and 4.0 per cent respectively. About 12 per cent of the total re-porting area is put to non-agricultural uses, e.g., settlement, roads, cemetery, guls (canals) and water bodies.

Cropping Patterns

Cropping pattern means the proportion of area under different crops at a point of time. The crop statistics published by the government are used to denote the cropping patterns. Cropping pattern is however, a dynamic con-cept as it changes in space and time. As stated at the outset, cropping structure of a region is the direct outcome of the physical, socio-cultural and historical factors.

Characterized with mountainous and undulating terrain and micro-level variations in temperature, precipitation and soils, the state of Jammu and Kashmir has a high degree of variation in its cropping patterns, crop combi-nation and crop diversification.

In general, the Jammu plain has a high concentration of wheat, rice, maize, pulses, fodder and oilseeds, while the Valley of Kashmir is well known for its paddy, maize, orchards (apples, al-mond, walnut, peach, cherry, etc.) and saffron cultivation. In Ladakh, barley, wheat, maize, vegetables, barseem and fodder are the main crops. The area and percentage of the total cropped area in the state.

The maize is the first ranking crop in the state, occupying about one-third of the total cropped area. Rice with 28.58 per cent of the gross cropped area is the second most important staple crop, followed by wheat to which over 26 per cent of the total cropped area is devoted.

It is interesting to note that rice and maize are the two rival crops for the first ranking, in the different parts of the state. Depending on the rainfall conditions, the hectarages under rice and maize fluctuate substan-tially. Consequently, in some of the years maize ranks first, while in others, rice occupies the maximum hectarage of the total cropped area.

Out of these two staple food crops, rice has high concentration in the Kashmir Valley and wheat in the Jammu Plain. Wheat is mainly grown in the district of Kathua and Jammu, adjacent to the province of Punjab. Pulses, oilseeds, spices, fod-der and vegetables are the other crops grown in the state.

Ranking of Crops

In any scheme of agricultural regionalisation, the ranking of crops has great significance. The ranking of crops not only gives an idea about dominant crops of a region, it also helps in knowing the crops which are competing for area with each other.

Second Ranking Crops

The second ranking crops. There are three crops namely; maize, rice and wheat which get second rank in the various districts of the state. The districts of the Kashmir Division excepting Kupwara, maize is the second ranking crop. In Kupwara rice gets second rank in area. In the district of Kathua and Jammu, rice is the second ranking crop, while in the remaining districts of the state wheat stands second.

Crop Combinations

Crops are generally grown in combination, and it rarely happens that a particular crop occupies a position of total isolation from other crops in a given region at a given point of time. The distribution maps of individual crops are interesting and useful for planner and policy-makers, but it is even more important to view the integrated assemblage of the various crops grown in a region.

For example, the demarcation of Jammu Division into wheat region does not explain the agriculturally significant fact that the re-gion under question has also rice and maize crops. For a comprehensive and clear understanding of the cropping mosaic of an agricultural region it is im-perative to delineate crop combination regions.

For the demarcation of crop combinations regions of the Jammu and Kashmir state, the standard deviation technique, advocated by Weaver was adopted and the resultant crop combinations.

It may also be observed from the figure that monoculture is not practised in the state. The given crops make only two and three crop combinations.

The two-crops combination is found in the Baramulla, Badgam, Kup-wara and Srinagar districts of Kashmir in which rice and maize are the constituent crops. In Kargil and Leh districts of Ladakh, millets and wheat are making two-crops associations.

The three-crops combination is found in six districts, namely, Anant-nag, Baramula, Ganderbal, Badgam, Srinagar and Pulwama of the Kashmir Division in which rice, maize and oilseeds enter into combination, and Kathua, Jammu and Udhampur of the Jammu Division. In the Districts of Jammu Division, wheat, maize and rice are the constituent crops of three crop combination.

As stated in the preceding paragraphs, the cropping patterns and crop as-sociation in the various districts of the state are closely influenced by the terrain, soil and extreme climatic conditions. In fact, in the Valley of Kash-mir and in the hilly districts of the state, severe winters do not permit the cultivation of rabi crops. Consequently, the farmers are not diversifying their cropping pattern.

The cereal crops which enter into crop combinations are grown mainly for the family consumption except wheat in Karhua and Jammu districts. The less number of crops entering into combinations, how-ever, should be considered as an indicative of the market-oriented cultivation of cereal crops as it is in the states of Punjab and Haryana. The agriculture, (excluding orchard and saffron) is by and large subsistent in character over the greater part of the state.

Double Cropped Area

Out of the total area sown (1074 thousand hectares) about 730 thousand hec-tares or 68 per cent was double cropped area in the state in 1994-95. The undulating and mountainous topography, harsh winters and inadequacy of irrigation in Ladakh and Kandi tracts are the main obstacles in the intensification of agriculture.

Consequently, the double and multiple cropped area is largely confined to the plain areas of Jammu Division and the valley floor of the Kashmir. In Ladakh, cultivation of crops is possible in only those tracts where irrigation facilities are available.

The districts of Anatnag, Pulwama, Jammu, Udhampur, Kathua, and Rajauri are the main areas in which double cropped area exceeds 70 per cent. In rest of districts the double cropped area is less than 10 per cent which shows a poor state of agricultural development.

The development of irrigation in the Kandi areas and cultivation of short duration crops in the Valley of Kashmir may enhance the double cropped area substantially, thereby making agriculture a more remunerative occupation.

Size of Holdings

The size of holdings of the Jammu and Kashmir state at the district level. About 74 per cent of the total holdings in the state are below one hectare and 25.14 per cent are between one and five hectares. There are only 225 farmers who have over 20 hectares of land each. The large holding farmers are confined to the hilly and moun-tainous tracts of Anantnag, Jammu, and Leh.

The district-wise analysis of size of holdings show that in the district of Srinagar about 95 per cent of the total holdings are below one hectare, while in Budgam and Kupwara districts over 85 per cent of the holdings are below one hectare. The size of holdings in Baramulla District is also very small as about 81 per cent are below one hectare. In the remaining districts 54 to 78 per cent of holdings are below one hectare.

The farmers who are having holdings between 1 to 5 hectares vary between 13 per cent in Pulwama District to 44 per cent in Rajauri District. The size of holdings on the whole is small except in the undulating moun-tainous tracts. The small size of holdings and the fragmented fields have adversely affected the productivity of arable land in most of the districts.

In the state of Jammu and Kashmir land reform measures were initiated, completed and implemented in the early years of 1950. It is, however, unfor-tunate, that land reforms in the state were restricted only to the redistribution of surplus land among the landless labourers and tenant form-ers.

The other attributes of land reforms such as agricultural extension service, education, supply of modern inputs, development of institutional credits and marketing, etc., were not accompanied by the redistribution of land to the tillers. This has adversely influenced the agricultural production and the economic prosperity of the farmers.

The small size of holdings and the non-availability of costly inputs to the small and marginal farmers have constrained innovations diffusion in their holdings as a result of which they, by and large, are the subsistent farmers.

The cereals like rice, wheat and maize dominate the cropping mosaic and in the kharif and rabi seasons and the non-cereals and coarse grains occupy an insignificant hectar-age. The predominance of staple food crops in the cropping patterns shows that agriculture in the state is, by and large, subsistent in character and most of the farmers generally grow crops for the family consumption.

Production of Food Grains

Jammu and Kashmir is essentially a grain growing state. Rice, maize, wheat, millets, and pulses are its major food crops. The growth trend of these crops. The total production of food grains in 1964-65 which was 9,827 thou-sand quintals, rose to 13575 thousand quintals in 1994-95, recording an increase of about 38 per cent. The production of wheat has gone up three times and there is 33 per cent increase in the production of rice, while maize recorded an increase of only 16 per cent over the period of last 30 years.

The area under commercial crops in each district of the state. Valley of Kash-mir commercial crops occupy over 20 per cent of the agricultural land except in Badgam in which this is 16 per cent. Pulwama District with 37 percent, has the highest hectarage under commercial crops. In the Jammu Division 2 to 7 percent of the arable and is under commercial crops.

Land-Man Ratio

The size of holding and fragmentation of fields have a direct bearing on agri-cultural practices, cropping patterns and yield per unit area. In Jammu and Kashmir like other parts of India, the land-man ratio is very low. The law of succession results in the subdivision and fragmentation of holdings. Consequently, the land-man ratio is declining fast. The cultivated area available per head of population.

The land-man ratio in all the dis-tricts of Jammu and Kashmir is below one acre except the Kathua District in which it is 1.55 acre per head of population. In the Kargil and Leh districts the cultivated area available per head of population in 0.38 and 0.57 hectare respectively.

The meagre cultivated land available per head of population in Ladakh is mainly because the land is mostly barren and the cli-mate is harsh and arid. Under the increasing pressure of population the land-man ratio is declining at a faster pace. If the present trend in the growth of population continues, the cultivated land available per head of population will be just half to that of the present one after 25 years.

Apiculture

Apiculture is also known as bee-keeping. In bee-keeping, bee-colonies are maintained for commercial production of honey and other by-products. Bee-keeping also helps in cross-pollination of crops. Honey produced by honeybees has been considered as a balanced and delicious food for thousands of years. In fact, honeybee is amongst the most ancients of domestic crea-tures.

The Valley of Kashmir is well known for its great diversity of flowers, ranging from lily to roses and saffron. Most flowers are dependent on bees for carrying pollens from the anthers (male part) of one flower to stigmas (female part) of the flower. Many fruit trees like almond, cherry, peach, pear, pumpkin and walnut do not produce fruits unless bees are present to pollinate them.

Bee-keeping is a household industry in the Valley of Kashmir. There are numerous bee-keeping places in Pampore, Srinagar, Pulwama, Tral, Kulgam, Badgam, Anantnag

(Islamabad), Qazigund, Kupwara and Karnah. In Jammu Division bee-keeping is being carried on in Udhampur, Poonch, Kishtwar, Bhadarwah, Batote, Ramban, Doda and Banihal.

Fisheries

The state of Jammu and Kashmir has enormous potential for the develop-ment of fisheries. The Valley of Kashmir abounds in numerous water bodies like lakes, ponds, wetlands, springs, streams and rivers. These waters are gen-erally alkaline in nature and are suitable for the culture of local as well as exotic fish.

The local fish fauna contains 30 species of which only a few are commercially important. Trout, common crop have been introduced into the valley during the present century. Fish-catching is done by the indige-nous technique of cast and dip nets. Long lines are also used in some waters.

Fish, the poor-man's protein forms an important item of diet of the local population of Kashmir. There is a continuous demand for the fish from the defence personnels stationed in the valley. The Wular, Manasbal, Dal, Anchar lakes and the Jhelum and its tributaries are the main sources of fish.

In 1965-66 the total produc-tion of fish was 42770 quintals which increased to 1,39,800 quintals in 1995-96. It is interesting to note that the share of Kashmir Division in the to-tal catch in 1995-96 was about 98.71 per cent and the remaining 1.29 per cent is the share of Jammu Division.

The various types of fish found in the valley are Punjabi-gad, Raput-gad, Star-gad, Algad, Chiroo, Kasher-gad, Dap-gad, Chush, Khrong, Guran, Trout, and Anur. Fish culture is being carried on in some of the water bod-ies of Kashmir. Trout culture is an important economic activity in the valley.

It was in the year 1901 that Mitchel procured eyed ova of trout fish from the Great Britain. It was at his initiative that a hatchway was started at Harwan in a stream. The eyed ova was spread to other streams like the Mad- humati, the Dachigam, Nala, and Pohru River.

Since the required conditions for trout culture are very exacting, the number of hatcheries is limited. The main trout hatcheries in Srinagar Dis-trict are Laribal, and Harwan. Besides the above hatcheries, there is a large trout farm at Achabal in the Anantnag District.

The production from these hatcheries is not sufficient to commercialize the sale of trout. Solman fish from Canada has also been brought and intro-duced in some of the water bodies of Kashmir. In brief, there is a great scope for the development of fisheries in the state of Jammu and Kashmir. The local and exotic fish need to be properly diffused in the different water bodies of the state.

Livestock

The state of Jammu and Kashmir has an agrarian economy. There is a close relationship between cultivation of crops and raising of livestock. In fact, both these activities are interdependent and complimentary to each other. The cool climate, the alpine pastures, abundance of fodder and constantly in-creasing demand of milk and milk products, all favour the keeping of cattle in Jammu and Kashmir state.

Cattle, sheep, goats, horses and ponies are kept and reared in large number in Jammu and Kashmir and Leh, is well known for the production of fine wool. The Ladakhi population is largely depend-ent for their sustenance on livestock, sheep and goats.

The total number of livestock in the state in 1990 was 78.95 lakh, out of which about 38 per cent were cattle, 32.30 per cent sheep and about 19 per cent goats. Buffaloes and horses, etc., constituted about 8 and 1.77 per cent of the total livestock respectively. The predominance of cattle population is found in the districts of Udhampur, Doda, Kathua, Anantnag, Baramulla, Pulwama and Rajauri.

The average livestock per household in the various districts of the state. It may be observed the dis-trict of Kargil (Ladakh) has the highest number of livestock per household being 20.

It is followed by Ladakh and Kupwara in which this ratio is 13 livestock per household.

The lowest number of livestock per household is in Srinagar and Jammu, being only about 2 and 4 respectively while in the re-maining districts this ratio varies between 4 to 10. Most of the livestock is however, local and inferior. The state government has been tak-ing a number of steps to improve the quality of cattle, sheep, goats and ponies. A number of cattle breeding centres have been established by the state government.

Some of the important cattle breeding centres are:

(i) Cattle Breeding Farm, Chashma-Shahi, and Manasbal, Srinagar.

(ii) Cattle Breeding Farm, Belicharna, Jammu.

(iii) Cattle Breeding Farm, Changspa.

(iv) Cattle cum Karakul Sheep Farm, Khumbathang.

(v) Yak Breeding Farm, Nubra, and

(vi) Veterinary Hospital, Dras.

For the development of better breeds of sheep, the Australian and Rus-sian Marino-sheep breeds were selected for Kashmir, and 16 sheep breeding farms with a total capacity of housing 1900 sheep were established in the dif-ferent sheep belts.

These sheep farms have been located in the areas where grazing facilities are available. In the course of breeding programmes, a new breed of sheep known as Kashmiri Merino has been developed with known body weight (average about 54 kg at the age of two and a half years).

In order to improve the quality of sheep, fine woolled sheep have been imported in piece-meal consignments from abroad. This exotic stock of sheep has been multiplied at sheep breeding farms and the quality Rams have been distributed.

Their distribution has resulted into cross-breed population of 8 lakh up till 1995. This cross-breed has been examined and it has been found that they have finer quality of wool and increase in mutton as com-pared to the local population.

Hydel Power and Energy Resources

Energy resources hold the key to the economic development of a geographic region. Their availability accelerates growth and development, while their non-availability retards the process of development. The level of consump-tion of energy in any country is a significant indicator of development.

For instance, the U.S.A. claims a per capita consumption of about 9,000 units per day. In sharp contrast, the Indian average per capita consumption is only 130 units. In Jammu and Kashmir, it is only 90 units per head per day.

Thus, it is one of the most backward states of India and may continue to stay as such unless adequate and early steps are taken to improve its power situ-ation. In the following paragraphs an attempt has been made to present a succinct picture of the energy resources of the state of Jammu and Kashmir. The state of Jammu and Kashmir though poor in coal, petroleum and natural gas, has tremendous potential for hydel power generation which has been inadequately tapped.

The three perennial rivers—Indus, Jhelum, and Chenab and their tribu-taries which drain the state, open immense opportunities for the generation of hydroelectricity. It has been estimated that these rivers provide theoreti-cally a potential of about 13,000 MW of hydel generation. Because of faulty planning and priorities, only a fraction of this potential has so far been util-ized.

The total hydel power generation in the state amounts to 168 MW in the summer season, while it drops to 121 MW in the winter season. In addition, the state gets 69 MW from the northern Grid which, with the help of capacitator, is raised to 75 MW. These sources of power together supply an average 956 MU of power per year which is almost half the actual de-mand for power in the state.

Lack of adequate power supply has retarded the growth of industrial, commercial and agricultural development in the state. Power supply is ra-tioned throughout the year and particularly during the winter season, when in Srinagar (capital) no part of the city gets more than 10 hours of power supply in 24 hours.

On account of this restricted supply of power in the state, and especially in the valley, no major industry, except the Hindustan Machine Tools (HMT) could so far be attracted despite packages of incen-tives, such as tax concessions and rent-free land, which the state government has offered to provide. If this gap in the demand and supply is allowed to grow, the state will perpetually remain one of the least developed states of India.

Hydel Power Projects under Investigation and Execution

Although, theoretically the potential for power development seems to be co-lossal, a realistic estimate of the potential for power development reveals that by the end of present century, if financial resources are made available and political stability restored, about 3200 MW hydel power may be installed in the state. The expected installed capacity of the three regions of the state.

The projects which have been taken up for investigation and execution in the Kashmir and Ladakh di-visions are either medium or mini-order projects. Such projects can be completed within the stipulated time, if funds are made available. In contra-diction, most of the projects in Jammu Division are large-sized and highly capital intensive.

The power development programmes in the early stages of the plan periods were installed because of the emphasis of state planners on major hydel projects, such as Salal and Dulhasti, which if completed would have yielded over 500 MW of power.

Unfortunately, the planning Commis-sion could not allocate requisite resources for these projects. In order to accelerate the process of development and to remove back-wardness, resources must be found to implement these power projects which are either in advanced stages of investigation or execution.

Power Demand and Supply Projections

The state of Jammu and Kashmir has a weak statistical base. Time series data are not available for scientific projection of power demands for the next 20 years by the various sectors of economy.

The unstable political conditions of the state especially that of the Valley of Kashmir are the main barriers in making reliable projections.

Even the present consumption figures for the various sectors are not available and have been disaggregated in accordance with the growth estimate of power demand projected by the state government. These points may be borne in mind while having a glance at reading, giving existing and projected power consumption in the state by 2000 A.D.

The energy planners of the state have projected a five-fold increase in the consumption of power, excluding domestic consumption from 956 MU in 1984 to nearly 5000 MU in 2000 A.D.

The highest rise in demand has been projected in the industrial sector on the assumption that a high rate of industrial growth is inevitable to cope with the rising unemployment.

Indus-trial growth will be dependent on the availability of power and the political stability.

The domestic sector is also likely to register phenomenal growth if other sectors develop along the lines projected above. The projection figures make it declare that economic well-being and future prosperity are inextrica-bly tied with massive power development.

Rural Electrification

Rural electrification is a pre-requisite for an integrated and sustainable devel-opment. The lifestyle in the rural areas goes under radical transformation once electricity is provided. Being hilly and mountainous and drained by perennial rivers, the state is favourably placed from the point of view of hydel power.

Unfortunately, the full potential of hydel power has not been harnessed in the state. Consequently, there is an inadequate supply of power in the months of December, January, and February, when the winters are snowy and severe.

The villages of Kashmir Division are electrified except Kupwara in which only 85 per cent villages are electrified and Baramulla in which 95 per cent of the villages have elec-tricity.

Over 90 per cent of the villages of Kathua, Jammu and Udhampur have electricity, while in Doda and Rajauri 87 and 84 per cent of the villages are electrified respectively.

Most of the villages of Leh District and about 40 per cent villages in Kargil do not have electricity supply. The state government is making sincere efforts to provide electricity to each and every village, and it is hoped that by 2010 A.D. the entire rural settlement of state will have electricity supply.

Health Care

The average life in the state of Jammu and Kashmir is shorter as compared to the adjoining states of Punjab and Himachal Pradesh.

It may be partly be-cause of the physiological and environmental factors and partly because of the inadequacy of health care centres and family welfare schemes. The district-wise distribution of health care facilities.

The medical institu-tion is available to 2,000 of population. In the state, both medical and paramedical manpower fall grossly short of the officially recommended minimum norm. In the districts of Srinagar and Jammu, there is heavy pres-sure on medical institutions.

The hospitals and medical institutions of the Jammu and Srinagar cities are under great stress which deserve urgent atten-tion of the government. The last decade witnessed a stagnation in the hospital beds-population ratio. There are startling differences between rural and urban areas, pointing to the large urban bias in the provision of health-care infrastructure.

KASHMIR - AGRICULTURE

Background: The Department of Agriculture in Jammu and Kashmir State came into existence during the pre-independence era. Till the year 1981 there was a single Directorate of Agriculture for the whole State.The Department was assigned specific mandate to bring about increase in crop production in a planned way to feed its fast growing population. In the year 1981-82, separate Directorates of Agriculture were established for both Jammu as well as Kashmir Divisions due to diverse agro-climatic conditions prevailing in these Divisions. This facilitated formulation of policies and programmes aimed at optimization and rational utilization of land and water resources for sustained agricultural production. Initially the department was exercising jurisdiction in the following wide fields:

Agri Development and Extension

Development of Seed multiplication Programmes

Research on Agriculture.

Maintenance of Botanicals gardens and development of Poultry.

Development of Horticulture & Management of Rakhs and Farms.

With the passage of time some of the schemes like parks and gardens, Horticulture Development, Poultry Development got separated during the early sixties. Subsequent to 60's the department got tremendous expansion in various schemes under the agenda of crash Programmes, intensive agri production, drought prone area programme plant protection management and with particular attention to development area under vegetable development programme and involving high yielding varieties of paddy and cereal seeds, besides introduction of farm Machinery subsequently from machinery was withdrawn and a separate corporation namely AIDC came into existence during late 60's.

During April 1982, the department got bifurcated in to two directorates one each at provincial level of J&K State followed by another bifurcation in the form that all the research schemes of department were transferred to a new organization known as SKAUST J&K in the month of 08/1982.

The Department of Agriculture, Kashmir envisages to help growers in the filed of agriculture with:

Land being a limited resource, would continue to be under stress in future.

A very high priority will, therefore, be accorded to exploring possibilities and potentialities of crop diversification in different agroclimatic zones with a view to maximizing the return per unit area of the land to the farmer, consistent with ecological and environmental considerations.

In high cropping intensity areas including irrigated areas, knowledge intensive precision farming techniques shall be prescribed and promoted for adoption.

Use of hybrid varieties shall be encouraged in order to break yield barriers.

Farmers will be advised about suitable technological packages including choice of crops, varieties and the requisite inputs to ensure high productivity with elastic cropping mechanism. The pattern of incentives in these areas and input packages shall be reviewed and tailored to suit the changing needs.

In rain-fed areas, diversified and value-added agriculture system shall be advocated. Incentives and technical messages shall converge on promotion and adoption of the full package of recommended practices including the choice of crops and varieties, rain water management including in situ- moisture conservation, water harvesting and recycling. The principle of management on water- shed basis shall be adopted for this purpose.

Available surface and ground water resources shall be tapped through public and private investments with a focus on providing irrigation facilities for appropriate crops in Karewa areas.

Ground water resources shall be properly mapped with assistance from the concerned central agencies .Extensive awareness programme shall be planned and implemented for judici.ous and efficient use of irrigation water. Energy needs for ground water exploitation shall be met on priority under single window clearance. Existing canal systems will be brought under participatory irrigation management. Special incentives will be provided for popularization of water-harvesting structures, storage tanks, watersaving methods of irrigation like sprinkler, drip and underground pipelines.

Agro-met advisory services shall be initiated for all the agro-climatic zones covering medium and long range weather forecasts for timely operations, in co-ordination with the state

Agriculture universities and National Centre for Medium Range Weather Forecast.

Major thrust will also be laid on increasing farm power as a supplement and substitute to reduced availability of draught animals for farming operations. Appropriate energy efficient, user-friendly and sturdy implements suiting the suiting the needs of various regions shall be developed and popularized.

Stress will be laid on quality at all stages of farm operations from sowing to primary processing. Quality consciousness among farmers and agroprocessors will be promoted through effective use of the media and personal contact by the departmental functionaries and instituting a scheme of awards for recognizing outstanding performance.

Integrated Nutrient Management practices using chemical fertilizers in conjunction with organic resources like farm-yard manure, enriched compost bio-fertilizers and green manuring will be popularized. This will optimize crop production in irrigated as well as rain-fed areas, besides improving soil productivity.

Integrated Pest Management package will be popularized for adoption through special incentives. This would check the indiscriminate use of chemical pesticides and out-break of secondary pests, pollution in food materials and eco-system and add a new dimension of organic produce for promoting marketing of fruits and vegetables.

Farmers will also be educated about the concept of integrated development of their farm household by taking a holistic view of their assets and potential. For this purpose, bringing about convergence of various schemes for development of the rural sector will be a priority.

It is necessary to bring out proper convergence in the implementation of various schemes for upliftment of rural masses and poverty alleviation. Necessary intuitional mechanism will be devised to bring out the requisite convergence.

Jammu Division has a total geographical area of 26,293 sq. kms, which comprises about 12 percent of the total geographical area of the State. Land use statistics is, however, available for a total reported area of 17.94 lac Ha.(17940 sq.kms) as per village records. The net area under cultivation in this Division is 3.90 lac Ha. out of which an area of 1.00 lac Ha. is irrigated.

Jammu Division - Physiography

Jammu Division is located between an altitude of 300 meters and 4200 meters above Mean Sea Level(MSL). Ranbirsingh Pura in Jammu district and Sumcham (Padder) in Doda district are the lowest and highest permanent settlement points for human population. Settlement pattern is mostly gregarious. Human population of the Division as per Census 2001 is 43.96 lacs. In physiography , following broad physical divisions are generally recognized from agricultural point of view :

Subtropical Zone: It spreads between an altitude of 300 meters and 1000 meters above MSL and enshrines Jammu district as a whole and parts of Kathua, Udhampur and Rajouri districts. This zone is characterized by hot summer, heavy summer monsoon and relatively dry but pronounced winter with pre-ponderance of alluvial soils. Normal summer monsoon ranges between 1200 to 1500 mm from mid June to mid September. This zone is further divided into two sub zones comprising the following areas :

Irrigated Sub-tropical Zone: It includes irrigated areas of Kathua, Barnoti, Hiranagar, Ghagwal, Samba, Vijaypur, Purmandal,Satwari, Bishnah, R.S. Pura, Marh & Bhalwal, Blocks on the right hand side of Jammu -Pathankot National Highway and Akhnoor, Khour, Nowshera, and Sunderbani Blocks on the Jammu - Poonch Highway

Unirrigated Sub-tropical Zone: It includes Kandi and unirrigated areas of Kathua, Barnoti, Hiranagar, Ghagwal, Samba & Purmandal to the left hand side of Jammu-Pathankot National Highway and Bhalwal, Akhnoor,Khour and parts of Kalakot, Nowshera and Sunderbani Blocks on Jammu-Poonch Highway and Ramban in Doda district

Most of the canal irrigation system being located in the Sub tropical zone, production and productivity of crops is high in this zone. The aromatic rice crop "Basmati" is also a speciality of the RS Pura, Bishnah, Satwari and Marh blocks of this zone and has high export value.

Intermediate Zone: This zone is located between an altitude of 1000 meters and 1500 meter above MSL. It consists of some parts of Basholi, Billawar, Ramnagar, Udhampur, Reasi, Pouni, Chenani ,Panchari, Ghordi, Mahore, Gool and large area of Kalakot, Budhal, Rajouri, Doda Darhal, Thathri, Balakot, , Ramsoo, Assar,Bhagwah, Ramban, Mahore, Mendhar, Poonch, Gordi, Panchari and Manjakot Blocks within the said altitude.

Barring some Blocks of Doda district i.e. Doda, Bhagwah, Assar and Ramban and some Blocks of Udhampur district i..e Mohre, Gool & Pouni which are drought prone, this zone has mild summer, fair monsoon during summer and relatively wet winter. Soils are spodosolic, undulating and prone to erosion.

Due to fair degree of monsoon and relatively wet & cool winters this zone has a fairly good level of productivity of Maize and Vegetable crops. In respect of Maize, an exceptionally high level of productivity (i.e.128 qtl/ha.)was obtained by a farmer in Rajouri district.

Temperate Zone: This zone includes all other areas of Jammu Division which are located above 1500 meters altitude. Of special mention are the Blocks of Warwan, Marwah,Dachhan, Chhatru, Paddar, Kishtwar, Thathri, Bhaderwah, Banihal, Mendhar, Manjakot, Bani, Basohli and parts of Bhagwah, Assar, Gool-Gulabgarh, Mahore,Dudu-Basantgarh, Darhal, etc.

This zone is characterized by relatively mild but dry summer with little monsoon and fairly cold- wet winter due to the 'Western Weather Disturbances'. It is mostly a monocropped zone with low production & productivity. However, other agriculture enterprises like pomology, apiculture & animal/ sheep husbandry are very common and rather supplement the modest agricultural income obtained through arable farming. The area is also suitable for seed production of temperate vegetable crops.

Saffron (Crocus sativus), possessing innumerable medicinal and aromatic properties is grown in the Kishtwar plateau of Doda district in an area of about 70 ha. Rajmash (Phaseolus vulgaris) possessing flavour and organo-leptic qualities having high market potential is also widely grown in the higher altitudes of this zone.

Climate: Jammu Division has a varied climate. Whereas it is hot in the sub-tropical belt during summer months, it is dry and cool in winter months. Intermediate zone has a mild climate both during summer as well as during winter. But in the temperate zone, whereas summer is mild and dry, winter is extremely cold & wet due to heavy snowfall.

INDUSTRIAL DEVELOPMENT

Though the state is comparatively backward in the industrial sector, there has been steady progress in the development of the small-scale sector, for which there is tremendous scope.

Jammu and Kashmir small -scale Industries Development Corporation Ltd. was started in 1975. The main objective of the corporation is to aid council, assist, finance, promote, and protect the interest of small-scale industrial units in the state.

J&K industrial and technical consultancy organisation Ltd. was set up in April 1997 as a subsidiary of Industrial Development Bank of India. The prime objective of J&K ITCO is to provide a package of consultancy service to tiny, small and medium scale industrial units, both existing and prospective as well as to render assistance to various state-level banks and institutions.

Some of the industries in the area include Hindustan Lever synthetic detergent plant, New Joinery Mill, cigarette factory and concrete factory at Bari-Brahamana industrial complex at Jammu.

Backward and hilly areas are receiving special attention with regard to the development of handloom weaving, leather tanning, and other local crafts. Trainees from these areas are receiving loans of Rupees 2000 each for installation of looms.

Their marketing problems are taken care of by the J&K small-scale Industrious Development Corporation. Carpet exports alone, earned for the country a foreign exchange of Rupees 13.20 crores in 1994-95.

Sericulture is one of the oldest industrious in the state. There are two big silk factories, one in Srinagar and another in Jammu. The major thrust is the production of quality cocoons for remunerative prices to the farmers. The Srinagar factory alone, manufactures about 300,000 meters of various types of silk fabrics, georgette, parachute and suiting. The Government woollen mills at Srinagar are another established manufacturing unit which has 2,018 woollen and 1,576 worsted spindles.

Handicrafts, being the traditional industry of the state, has been receiving top priority in view of its large employment potential and also demand of handicraft goods both within and outside the country. Handicraft production includes mainly papier mache, wood carving, carpets, shawl making, embroidery etc. This industry particularly in carpets, earns substantial foreign exchange.

The handloom development corporation is producing woollen items like tweed, blazer, blankets, shawls, dhusas, kani shawls, etc.

The setting up of the Hindustan Machine Tools Units has been a pace-setter for the large-scale industrialisation of the state. Both the Hindustan Machine Tools (HMT) and Indian Telephone Industries have expanded and diversified their production at Srinagar - their annual total production having since crossed Rupees 201 crores. The Jammu region is not lagging behind. Three rosin and turpentine factories were set up at the Bari-Brahamana complex in the private sector and also a modernised rosin and turpentine factory at Miran sahib in the Jammu division. Two slate pencil manufacturing units and wool combing project were commissioned at Bari - Brahamana.

Industrial activity is however, mostly concentrated in the two main cities -Srinagar and Jammu - and their surrounding areas. Determined efforts are made to decentralise industrial growth; this being the guiding principle in setting up of the district Industrious centre. A scheme for infrastructure development of industrial units has been formulated for Battal Balian and Udhampur at a cost of Rupees 5 crores.

Irrigation and Power

The state has an identified hydro potential of over 15,000 MWs (out of while hardly 10 percent has been harnessed till date). A major portion of this hydro potential, about 6,000 MWs is on the Chenab river which is veritable goldmine for the state. Kashmir province has an identified potential of about 2,000 MWs, out of which about 35 percent has been utilised so far. The Eighth Five year plan outlay for power sector stands at Rs.1175.48 crores. The installed power capacity by the end of March 1995 was 387.30 MWs with another 3.65 MWs added in 1995-96.

A provision for Rs.205.52 crores stands earmarked for irrigation and flood control including command area development programme of the state during the Eighth Five year plan. The area irrigated was 4.42 lakh hectares by 1994-95 ends.

With a view to tapping the available hydel potential, the state government is exploring the possibility of attracting private, both local and foreign, capital/assistance for taking up major hydel projects in the state. Upper Sindh hydel project is a major priority and it was commissioned by December 1998. The Salal hydel project with a capacity of about 345 MWs in the central sector is already in operation as is the Uri hydel project which accounts for 480 MWs of power. Another project is the Dulhasti project, accounting for 390 MWs.

During the current year power is available from Pahalgam hydel project (3 MW), Machhil hydel project (0.7 MW), Iqbal hydel project (1.25 MW), Huftal hydel project (1 MW) and Chenani-II / Seva-III (9 MW). During 1997-98, Zainakote grid station, 120 MVA stations at Kathua, Akhnoor, Rajouri and Ranbir Singh Pura were completed.

Another important project is the 450-MW Baglihar project on the Jammu-Srinagar national highway. This project can annually generate a total of 2,600 million units of energy.

Next project is the Kishenganga project in the Gurez valley. The annual generation from the project is 1,460 MWs.

The state has in the pipeline ten more attractive investigated projects which are: Uri (280 MW), Sewa-II (120 MW), Sawalkote (600 MW), Pakaldul (1,000 MW), Burser (1,020 MW), Parkhachak (60 MW), Ratle (170 MW), Naunatoo (400 MW), and Kirthai (750 MW) for implementation, with private investment, during the next fifteen to twenty years.

LAND REFORMS AND AGRICULTURE

Among the states of the Indian Union, the Jammu and Kashmir state had the unique distinction of having introduced land reforms of considerable magnitude. The salutary feature of the reforms introduced as a result of the enforcement of the Big Landed Estates Abolition Act 1950 was that as many as 9000 and some-odd landowners were expropriated from 1.82 lakh hectares of land and out of this, 0.94 lakh hectares of land were transferred in ownership rights to cultivating peasants free of any encumbrances. By far the most important step taken towards the implementation of this programme was the enactment of the Jammu and Kashmir Agrarian Reform which was amended in 1978. Under the measure absentee landlordism was completely abolished, and ceiling of 5.1 standard hectares fixed on agricultural land holdings excluding orchards in the state. The reform was bound to achieve the twin purpose of giving the cultivator his rightful place in the social order and also ensure more efficient utilisation of the state's resources.

The main objectives of the government's strategy are:

- Achieve self-sufficiency and self-reliance in terms of production of food grains
- To improve and augment the income levels of the farming community
- To ensure better income distribution and to reduce regional disparities.

The state is predominantly a mono-cropped and rainfed economy with about 40 percent of the area in Jammu division and 60 percent in Kashmir division having assured means of irrigation. Agriculture is one of the key factors and the mainstay of the state's economy. The productivity level of paddy at about 40 quintals per hectare in Kashmir valley is the highest in the country. Rice, maize, and wheat are the major crops.

While in the Kashmir region wheat, oil seeds and fodder cultivation is being introduced as a second crop, in Jammu, farmers are raising paddy as an additional crop. Still another innovation is the introduction of mushrooms. Of the produce, 90 percent is canned and exported from the state, under the guidance and supervision of the agriculture department.

Mushroom demonstration-cum-training centres have been established at Srinagar, Baramulla and Anantang districts and at Ranbir Singh Pura in the Jammu division. The World Bank has provided financial assistance to the state for developing mushroom cultivation on modern lines.

Agricultural production of the state has registered a steady growth. The state's foodgrain production is expected to increase to 22.59 lakh tonnes by the end of the Ninth plan as against 13.56 lakh tonnes at the end of the Eighth plan. A similar upward trend is discernible in regard to consumption of chemical fertilisers which has gone up from 43,400 metric tonnes to 72,400 metric tonnes during the same period. The average per hectare yield of rice has increased from 13.89 quintals in 1989-90 to 22.6 quintals in 1994-95. The average yield of maize and wheat per hectare has increased from 15.65 quintals and 11.50 quintals in 1989-90 to 18.71 quintals and 14.29 quintals, respectively in 1993-94.

There has been a major thrust on the seed production programme to deal with the specialised requirements of the agro-climatic zones of the state. The area under oil seeds has increased from 70,000 hectares in 1989-90 to 1.76 lakh hectares in 1994-95 and that of pulses from 40,000 hectares in 1989-90 to 81,000 hectares in 1994-95. Given the conducive climatic factors, saffron and zeera cultivation in the valley and doda has received a tremendous impetus. These crops have potentiality for earning foreign exchange for the country. The area under saffron has gone up from 4,000 hectares in 1989-90 to 4,383 hectares in 1993-94 with corresponding increase in production from 90.27 quintals to 130.65 quintals. The saffron production has been encouraged in the non-traditional areas.

The Sheri-i-Kashmir University of Agricultural Sciences And Technology, established in the year 1982, has created its own niche in purveying a strong training and research input, for promotion of agriculture and horticulture in the state. After assiduous research carried over years, the university has been able to evolve new varieties of rice and oil seeds, suitable for temperate areas.

Under the Intensive Agriculture programme, a number of high-yielding varieties of seeds have been tried and introduced to boost up agricultural production. The state's agricultural experimentation has borne fruit and two high-yielding varieties of rice, K-78 and K-84, suitable for high regions, were evolved. Paddy has been cultivated in higher reaches of the valley which experience early snowfall.

Increasing agricultural production through extension of irrigation is part of the basic agricultural strategy. A number of irrigation projects such as the remodeling of the Ranbir Canal, the Pargwal Canal and the Udhampur Canal in the Jammu division, have been completed.

The Ravi-Tawi irrigation complex symbolizes execution of the grand concept of using to the last drop of the available water resources of all major rivers flowing in the Jammu division and harnessing in the service of agriculture by creating irrigation facilities for the arid and backward belt of the division.

Underground water resources are also being explored and exploited in the areas of the Jammu division where gravity schemes are not feasible. A new irrigation scheme, namely 'Igophy' has been introduced in Laddakh district. Special projects like multiple cropping schemes have caught on.

FORESTS

Kashmir, known all over the world as 'Paradise on the earth', has the finest forests in the country. The abundant forest wealth of the state is spread over 21,307 sq. km, which include 718.15 sq.km. of sanctuaries and game reserves. A rich variety of conifers such as fir pine, spruce, deodar, chir, kali, etc. grow in the forests. Special attention is being paid to the promotion of the forest research and preservation and making up the losses on the dwindling species.

The emphasis has been shifted from production to conservation and improvement of natural forests by bringing more areas under afforestation and under regular scientific management. During the Seventh plan, the amount of Rupees 3,882 lakhs was spent on the development of forests.

The Game Preservation Department has since been reoriented and the Central Wildlife Act was made applicable to the state with effect from January 1, 1979. The Act forbids illegal felling of trees and ensures the preservation of the ecological balance in the forests and the game sanctuaries like the one at Dachigan in Kashmir.

Forests, which constitute 14.50% of the state's total geographical area, play a key role in maintaining the ecological balance. The government has taken several measures for rehabilitation of degraded forests and also enlisted public cooperation in it. The use of forest land for non-forestry purposes has been prohibited by the Forest Conservation Act in 1992. The World Bank-aided Social Forestry Project launched in 1982-83 has helped in raising plantations on a massive scale.

A new concept of Joint Forest Management (JFM) has been introduced and village forest committees have been formed in 600 villages. These committees are useful in preservation of forest wealth to a large extent. Nearly 7,000 hectares of state and forest land has also been covered under different soil conservation schemes during the first three years of the Eighth Five year plan.

SOCIAL WELFARE

The social welfare department of the state has been concentrating on the welfare of the so-called backward classes and other weaker section of the society. For imparting training to the member of the scheduled castes and the backward classes in weaving, leather technology, wood work, tailoring, knitting, and embroidery, the government has set up eight technical institutes in the state. The social welfare department is also running nearly 200 community social welfare centres in Jammu and in the Kashmir division. There are two residential institutes for the blind, one each in the Jammu and Kashmir regions.

At present, many hostels are functioning in the state for providing free boarding, lodging, health care, and coaching facilities to the Gujjar and Bakarwal students. The national family planning Programme was started in 1957-58, and it was followed by the establishment of Regional Family planning Training Centre in 1967.

The welfare of government employees, especially at the lower rungs, is particularly looked after. Another aspect of welfare is the generation of the employment opportunities. Small -scale industrial units set up in far- flung areas under the rural Industrial Programme have a pronounced welfare bias. The units include handloom weaving, oil crushing, leather tanning, shoe-making, etc. Jammu and Kashmir has been declared as a special category state, on grounds of financial imbalances. The ratio of grant to loan is 90:10 in special category states as against 30:70 for the others.

TRANSPORT AND COMMUNICATION

In the landlocked state like Jammu and Kashmir, road transport is an indispensable means of communication for the regular distribution of essential and other commodities. Hence, the government has given the highest priority to the construction and maintenance of roads.

The railway line between Jammu and Udhampur, started in 1981-82, was completed by 1997-98. Rs.142 crores, with an addition of another Rs.50 crores have been spent on completing it. This railway line has been further extended up to Srinagar at an additional cost of Rs.1, 900 crores.

Economic development of the state and access to the landlocked and unexposed areas are dependent on roads. The total road length was 13,540 Kms by March 1996. Of the 6,268 villages in the state, 3,962 villages were connected through roads by 1995. By the Eighth plan, 228 additional villages are likely to be connected through the roads.

An alternative to the existing national highway connecting Jammu and Srinagar, known as the Mughal road was completed by Ninth plan period. The Ministry of Surface Transport has sanctioned Rs.25 lakhs under the National Patrolling scheme for the purpose of an ambulance and crane for deployment on the highway.

In the Kashmir valley, timber bridges constructed decades ago are being replaced and reconstructed by concrete bridges. The major bridges completed in 1995 were Abdullah Bridge, Aishmuquam, and Larkipora in Kashmir valley and Kathua Bridge in Jammu division. Other bridges under construction are Pul-Doda Bridge in Doda, Sher-i-Kashmir Bridge, Poonch fly-over project, Jammu, Wagoora, Vailoo, Hillar, Pahoo and Biddar Bridges in the valley and Kali Dhar Bridge in Rajouri district.

Communication facilities have considerably expanded with the opening of new telephone exchanges, extension of existing lines and the establishment of direct-dialing services between Srinagar and Jammu, Srinagar and Delhi and between Srinagar, Anantnag and Baramulla. This service has been extended upto Mumbai and other important towns in the country.

A new radio transmitter of much greater power has since been installed in Jammu, and the Srinagar station has been further strengthened. A radio station has since been set up in Leh. The TV station in Srinagar, catering to a population of 20 lakhs, has become very popular. Similar is the case with the Jammu TV station.

A yard-com-workshop complex at Srinagar has been constructed involving a cost of Rupees 4.70 crores.

TRANSPORT AND MEANS OF COMMUNICATIONS

Geographical factors govern transport and means of communication in Kashmir. Although there has been great progress in transport and communication system in the valley, man is still the beast of burden in some mountainous areas. In the valley roads are the main means of transportation for wheeled traffic. The Government of India, in order to make the traffic possible between the valley of Kashmir and the rest of the country even in the coldest weather of the year, has constructed two tubes of Jawahar Tunnel near Banihal at a height of 2200 metres above sea level Rivers in the valley of Kashmir are also navigable. On the higher altitudes, where roads are not so common, mules and ponies are also used as means of transportation. There is also Air transport from Jammu to Srinagar and Laddakh.

Road Transport in Kashmir

1. Jhelum Valley Road is 132.5 Kms. long and connects Srinagar, Pattan, Baramula, Mohra and Uri. It is also a part of the National Highway and is very important from military point of view.
2. Srinagar-Shopian Road is 53 Kms. long and connects Srinagar, Pampore, Pulwama, and Shopian.
3. Srinagar-Kulgam Road connects Srinagar, Khannabal and Kulgam. It is 71 Kms. long.
4. Srinagar-Gulmarg Road is 29 Kms. long and connects Srinagar, Tangmarg and Gulmarg.
5. Srinagar-Pahalgam Road is 96.5 Kms. long and connects Srinagar, Awantipura, Khannabal, Mattan, Aishmuqam and Pahalgam. From Pahalgam a bridle path leads to Swami Amarnath cave which is 45 Kms. from Pahalgam. On this route, Chandanwari, Sheshnag and Panjtarni stations are worth mentioning.

6. Srinagar-Bandipur Road leads to Shalateng- situated on the Jhelum Valley Road. From Shaltang this road leads to Bandipur. It is 56Kms. long. From Bandipur to Sopore it is 33 Kms. From Bandipur another road leads to Gurez and it serves as a military defence road.
7. Srinagar-Wayal Road is 85 Kms. in lengh. On this route, Anantnag, Achhabal, Kukarnag are worth mentioning.
8. Sopore-Tetwal Road is 95 km, long and connects Sopore, Handwara Trehgam, Chowkibal, Santochangli and Tetwal. From Srinagar to Chowkibal the road is open for both public and military traffic, but from Chowkibal to Tetwal only military vehicles run and the road is closed during winter when there is heavy snowfall.
9. Srinagar-Gandarbal-Baltal Road winds its way across the Anchar Lake passing through Ganderbal where the Sindh Nullah enters the Anchar Lake. This road connects with many other roads, the important one is Khirbhawani or Tulamula road leading to the well known shrine. The main road passes through the entire valley of the Sindh Nullah upto Baltal, the foot of the Zojila pass Beyond Baltal the road leads to Matayan and to Dras. It is 117 Kms. long up to Baltal and from Baltal to Dras it is 45 Kms.
10. Srinagar-Charar-e-Sharif Road has been constructed over the karewa to the southeast. It leads to the well known shrine Chrar-e-Sharif.
11. Srinagar-Laddakh Road is 80 Kms from Srinagar to Sonamarg. It connects Srinagar, Gandarbal and Sonamarg, from where after passing over the Zojila Pass it connects Machai, Drass, Kargal and Leh, the capital of Laddakh Province. From Sonamarg to Leh the distance is 350 Kms.
12. Kargal-Askardu Road is 151 Kms. in length. On the way, Kharalpul, Awiding, Bagicha Talse, Madhopore, Gole and Theggo are worth mentioning.

13. Pulwama-Yus-gogji Pathar Road connects Pulwama, Parkota, New Kalipora, Ramopakherapora, Kanidanwan and Yus-gogjipathar.

Other important road- links are:

14.	Khannabal-Kulalgam	17 Kms.
15.	Anantnag-Verinag	26 Kms.
16.	Srinagar-Tral -Shikargah	45 Kms.
17.	Shopian-Kulgam	22 Kms.
18.	Shopian-Wuyun-Letapore	31 Kms.
19.	Shopian-Bijhebara	31 Kms.
20.	Srinagar-Naseem-Pandach	18 Kms.
21.	Srinagar-Halwar-Drafama	27 Kms.
22.	Srinagar-Aerodrome	11 Kms.
23.	Srinagar-Chrar-e-sharif-Yusmarg	47 Kms.
24.	Srinagar-Badgam-Raithan	32 Kms.
25.	Baramula-Langet-Handwara	29 Kms.
26.	Srinagar-Sopore	73 Kms.
27.	Srinagar-Sopore-Gangbug	137Kms.
28.	Handwara-Nichhama	21 Kms.
29.	Handwara-Magam-Lonawara	27 Kms.
30.	Ukherhal-Senawatipul	11 Kms.
31.	Srinagar-Panthchak-Lethpora	31 Kms.

7

Tourism

INTRODUCTION

Skiing is popular in Gulmarg, showing cable car in a snow-clad mountain.

Before the insurgency intensified in 1989, tourism formed an important part of the Kashmiri economy. The tourism economy in the Kashmir valley was worst hit. However, the holy shrines of Jammu and the Buddhist monasteries of Ladakh continue to remain popular pilgrimage and tourism destinations. Every year, thousands of Hindu pilgrims visit holy shrines of Vaishno Devi and Amarnath, which has had significant impact on the state's economy. It was estimated in 2007 that the Vaishno Devi yatra contributed 4.75 billion (US$66 million) to the local economy annually a few years ago. The contribution should be significantly greater now as the numbers of Indian visitors have increased considerably. Foreign tourists have been slower to return. The British government still advises against all travel to Jammu and Kashmir with the exception of the cities of Jammu and Srinagar, travel between these two cities on the Jammu-Srinagar highway, and the region of Ladakh, while Canada excludes the entire region excepting Leh.

Besides Kashmir, several areas in the Jammu region have a lot of tourist potential as well. Bahu Fort in Jammu city is the major attraction for the tourists visiting that city. Bage-e-Bahu is another tourist destination. The local aquarium, established by the fisheries department, is visited by many. Tourists from across India visit Jammu in a pilgrimage to Mata Vaishno Devi. Mata Vaishno Devi is located in the Trikuta Hills, about 40 to 45 km from Jammu City. Approximately 10 million Pilgrims visit this holy place every year.

Tourism in the Kashmir valley has rebounded in recent years, and in 2009, the state became one of the top tourist destinations of India. Gulmarg, one of the most popular ski resort destinations in India, is also home to the world's highest green golf course. The state's recent decrease in violence has boosted the economy and tourism. It was reported that more than a million tourists visited Kashmir in 2011.

LAKES

The paradisiacal beauty of Kashmir valley can be mainly attributed to its outlandish natural beauty, pretty landscape and beautiful water bodies. These water bodies are of great ecological and socioeconomic significance. The most famous of these are Dal Lake and Nagin Lake of Srinagar with their multi-faceted eco-system and grandeur. National and international tourists throng to the place attracted by the breathtaking beauty of the places.

Dal Lake: Described as the Lake Par Excellence by Sir Walter Lawrence, Dal Lake of Srinagar is the jewel in the crown of the Kashmir. Majestic mountains surround its three sides. It houses the world famous Shikaras and Houseboats, which afford an opportunity to tourists to reside on the lake in an atmosphere of peace and tranquility. Dal Lake changes its moods and scenery throughout the day and after every few kilometres.

It is lined with world famous Boulevard road. One of the most beautiful lakes of India and the second largest in the J&K state, the shores of Dal Lake is clustered with sloping roofed houses on islands, while other parts appear lush and green like well-tended gardens. The campus of University of Kashmir is also located along the shores of the lake.

Nagin Lake: Leading from the Dal is the smaller Nagin Lake. Trees of willow and poplar whose reflection is mirrored in the lake edge the waters. One can hire Bathing Boats here, as well as on the Dal along with the exciting water-skis and motor launches. There are Shikaras to be hired for an unbelievably romantic experience. The lake lies to the east of the city at the foot of the Zabarwan Mountain. To its south is the Shankaracharya hill (or Takht-i-Sulaiman) and to the west, is Hari Parbat.

VAISHNO DEVI

Vaishno Devi Mandir is one of the holiest Hindu temples dedicated to Shakti, located in the hill of Vaishno Devi, Jammu and Kashmir, India. In Hinduism, Vaishno Devi, also known as Mata Rani and Vaishnavi, is a manifestation of the Mother Goddess.

The temple is near the town of Katra, in Udhampur district in the state of Jammu and Kashmir,. It is one of the most revered places of worship in Northern India. The shrine is at an altitude of 5200 feet and a distance of approximately 12 kilometres (7.45 miles) from Katra. Million of pilgrims visit the temple every years and is the second most visited religious shrine in India, after Tirupati Balaji Mandir. The Shri Mata Vaishno Devi Shrine Board maintains the shrine. A rail link from Udhampur to Katra is being built to facilitate pilgrimage.

Legend: According to Hindu mythology, Bhairav Nath, a selfish demon, chased a young girl named Vaishno Devi, whom he believed was an incarnation of the Mother Goddess. While running away from Bhairav, Devi shot an arrow into the Earth from which water gushed out. The resultant river is known as *Baanganga*. It is believed that by taking a bath in Baanganga (Baan: Arrow), a believer of the Mother Goddess can wash away all his sins. The banks of the river, known as *Charan Paduka*, are marked by Devi's foot imprints, which remains intact till date. Vaishno Devi then took shelter in a cave known as Garbh Joon near *Adhkawari* where she meditated for 9 months attaining spiritual wisdom and powers. Her meditation was cut short when Bhairav located her. Vaishno Devi was then compelled to take the form of Maha Kali when Bhairav tried to kill her. The manifestation of the Mother Goddess took place at the mouth of the Holy cave at Darbar. The Goddess then beheaded Bhairav with such sheer force, that his skull fell at a place known as *Bhairav Ghati*, 2.5 km. from the Holy Cave.

In his dying moments, Bhairav pleaded for forgiveness. The Goddess knew that Bhairav's main intention in attacking her was to achieve salvation. She not only granted Bhairav liberation from the cycle of reincarnation, but also granted him a boon, whereby every devotee, in order to ensure completion of the pilgrimage, had to visit Bhairav Nath's temple near the Holy cave after the darshan of the goddess. Meanwhile Vaishno Devi assumed the shape of a rock with three pindis (heads) and immersed herself into meditation forever.

CHARAR-E-SHARIEF

Chrar-e-Sharief is a shrine revered by both Muslims and Hindus dedicated to Sheikh Nooruddin, who was arguably the greatest mystic-saint of Kashmir. The Islamic militants burned it down in 1995 at the behest of Pakistan. An example of the composite culture of Kashmir, the Sheikh was born as Nund Reshi or Sahazanand in 1377. His tale is full of wonders. His ancestors migrated from Kishtwar to the Valley. His father, Salar Sanz, who was a pious man, was influenced by the spiritual teachings of the Sufi Saint, Yasman Reshi, who arranged his marriage to Sadra Maji. It is said that for three days, the infant Nund refused to be breast-fed until on the third day, a Yogini (a well-known female saint), Lal Ded entered the house and fed the child her own milk. After that, she left the house prophesizing that the infant would be her spiritual heir.

While personifying the Hindu-Muslim culture of the Valley, Nund, was later named as Naruddin meaning 'the light of faith'. He fully believed in the immanence and transcendence of God and hoped for a society based on moral values and preached against indulgence. It is said that all his life he wore a coarse pheran and within two days of his death in 1438 at Charar, nine lakh people are said to have gathered at the Shrine, including the King, Sultan Zainul Abdin. The saint is known to have preached against communal hatred and in one of his teachings, he wrote: "We belong to the same parents. Then why this difference? Let Hindus and Muslims together worship God alone. We came to this world like partners. We should have shared our joys and sorrows together."

HARI PARBAT FORT

The Mughal fort situated on the banks of the Dal Lake of Srinagar, it is positioned on top of the Sharika Hill. Originally, it was built during the reign of Akbar but its present structure owes itself to the Afghan governor of Kashmir in the 18th century. It has a Parvati temple on the western slope and the Muslim shrines of Khwaja Makhdoom Sahib and Akhund Mullah Shah on the southern one. On the southern side of the outer wall there is a Guru Dwara, which commemorates the visit of Guru Hargobind Singh. Presently the fort is under army occupation. According to the local legend, this hill was once a lake as large as a sea and was inhabited by the abominable demon known as Jalobhava. The inhabitants called on Goddess Sati, spouse of Lord Shiva for her help. She took the form of a bird and dropped a pebble on the demon's head, which kept on increasing in size until the demon was crushed by it. Hari Parbat is revered as that pebble and it is said to have become the home for all 33 crore gods of the Hindu pantheon.

Another version of the myth that involves the hill, says that two demons, Tsand and Mond occupied the fair valley. Tsand conceded himself in water near the present location of Hari Parbat and Mond somewhere above the present Dal Gate. They were a menace to the people of the valley, which could not be inhabited owing to their dreaded presence. Thus, the gods invoked Goddess Parvati who assumed the form of a Hor (myna) and flew to Sumer from where she got a pebble in her beak and threw it on the demon Tsand to crush him.

The pebble grew into a mountain. She is worshipped as Sharika in Shri Tsakra (an emblem of cosmic energy pervading the universe) occupying the middle part of the western slope of the hill. The hill is also called Predemna Peet or Kohi Maran. Akbar the Great built the outer wall of the fort in 1590 at a cost of one crore and ten lakh of rupees. The inscription in Persian at the Kathi Darwaza commemorating this work can be read even today. Akbar intended to lay the foundation of a new capital inside the fort and call it Nagar Nagor. The ruins of certain terraces can still be seen on the side of the Pokhiri Bal. The views of the Dal Lake and a part of the valley from the fort are spectacular.

MARTAND SUN TEMPLE

The most memorable and beautiful work of King Lalitaditya is the construction of spacious Martand temple, which the emperor got built in honour of the Sun God or Bhaskar. Lalitaditya was a Kshatriya of Surya (Solar) dynasty. The style of the construction of the temple and the skill exhibited in its construction is rare in the history of the world. Though the cities, towns and the ruins belonging to the era of Lalitaditya are not to be found so easily, the remnants of the big Martand temple, which the emperor had built at the pilgrimage of the same name, is an example of unique building skill of ancient Hindus. They are praised for their design, beauty and art.

Martand holds a very high place in the world's great architectural designs and is considered to be not only an example of the Kashmiri architectural skill but also has pride of having been set up at a prettier spot than those of Parthinan, Taj Mahal and St. Peters. A representative of all such great buildings and monuments or a combination and sum total of all the qualities, the ruins of the huge temple stand in a square field with snowcapped mountains as its backdrop. This temple has been built with strong and square limestones and exhibits the pillars of Greek pattern. Martand temple is said to be a mirror of the art and skill of Kashmiri Hindus. This way Lalitaditya should not be considered only a founder of a vast empire but also a founder of art and skill of Kashmiri Hindus for six centuries.

SUDH MAHADEV TEMPLE

Situated in the town of Chanhani in the western part of the Jammu, the Sacred Temple of Sudhmahadev was constructed by Chaudhari Ramdas of Chanhani and his son Chaudhari Parag Mahajan about 80 years ago. Shri Masu Shahane of Sudhmahadev is said to have constructed the entrance door of the temple of Sudhmahadev. The holy spot near Patnitop, it is situated at an altitude of 1225 m above sea level. Pilgrims visit the shrine on the full moon night of the rainy season to worship the famous Trident and a mace, which is said to belong to Lord Shiva. The Devak stream originating at this place disappears magically among the rocks a few kilometres down stream. The temple has a natural black marble 'lingam' and Goddess Parvati mounted on Nandi. The 'Dhooni' (sacred fire) commemorates the spiritual attainments of Baba Roop Nath who is said to have attained Samadhi there. It is said to have been burning constantly ever since Baba Roop Nath is said to be residing in the temple.

According to a popular legend, it is believed that Lord Shiva who was in his Samadhi (deep meditation) shot his big Trishul (trident) to protect his consort Uma startled suddenly by her loud cry. However, it was Shiva's devotee, Sudheet who approached Uma to pay his respectful obeisance and since he was a demon in his previous birth, his demoniac looks frightened her and she made a loud shriek. The trident however killed Sudheet. Shiva realized his mistake and offered to resuscitate him but Sudheet preferred the death given by Lord Shiva Himself. Touched by his devotion, Lord Shiva prefixed his name to the place forever and the broken trident in three pieces, is still installed in the temple.

KASHMIR DAL LAKE

Dal Lake has rightfully become an icon of the Kashmir tourism industry. A Himalayan urban lake, it has five basins and a number of channels that are well linked with each other. There are plenty of fishes in Dal Lake and fishery is the second largest industry of the region centred on the lake. The sparkling quiet waters of Dal surrounded by snowcapped mountains on its three sides undoubtedly mark it as one of the most beautiful lakes of India. It is also the second largest lake in the State of Jammu and Kashmir with numerous gardens and orchards all along its shores. Houseboats form an indelible part of the scenery of the Dal Lake that are always ready to take tourists to a romantic and peaceful ride of the lake and soothe their nerves as the houseboat floats over the slightly rippling waters. They also offer some of the most exotic views of the splendid scenery of the Dal Lake.

There are Shikaras that look like small ornate versions of the gondolas of Venice that offers ferry rides to and from the banks of the lake to the houseboats. The shores of the Lake house the distinct Mughal monuments and the campus of the University of Kashmir while the two hillocks overlooking the lake house Shankaracharya and Hari Parbat temples.

The glorious Mughal gardens on its shores contribute to the beauty of the Dal Lake. Out of about five hundred gardens laid down in 16th to 17th century, only a few still survive. There have been controversies about the origin of the Dal Lake. While some geologists believe that the origins of Dal Lake lie in the Pleistocene Oligotrophic Lake that once covered the entire valley of Kashmir, others just believe it to be a flood plain lake. The floating gardens of Dal Lake are considered a beauty in themselves. One can find a number of restaurants and hotels at the lakefront that have sprung up, encouraged by the large influx of tourists here.

KASHMIR VALLEY

Perfection beyond this world makes Kashmir a paradise. The land of sparkling rivers and sleepy lakes, of startling gardens and regal Chinar trees, Kashmir boasts of some of the most beautiful flowering meadows and snowcapped peaks. The abundance of natural beauty has earned the valley a nickname of the 'Switzerland of the East'.

It is mesmerizing to see how this endless beauty never fails to charm the viewers with its changing scenes from dazzling white snow of winters to blooming fragrance of spring. The sparkling greenery of summers are welcome too as the flaming beauty of autumn. The art house of the Seasons, the beauty of Kashmir is complete to the giggling girls with fair Indian complexion and rosy cheeks and the exquisite handicrafts of the area.

Kashmir's Topography: The high snowcapped ridges of the Himalayan range in the east and the Pir Panjal range in the west and south enclose Kashmir. Jhelum River glides across Srinagar and swiftly flows through the winding ways of the valley. The geologists have confirmed the truth behind the popular belief that Kashmir was once a huge lake called the Karewa, which was formed by the blocking of the Jhelum River. However, the river formed a deep gorge through the Pir Panjal range at Uri and carved out its new way. Thus, the waters of the Karewa gradually drained away, leaving behind the stunning valley of Kashmir. One can still find corals and other marine fossils in this region.

The Glorious Name: There have been different versions of the legend behind the name of Kashmir. It is said that the great saint Kashyap Rishi went on a pilgrimage to the place. When he reached Naukabandan near Kaunsarnag, at the request of the people he killed Bahudev, the giant of Satisar and let the water of the lake flow out near Baramulla. Thus, the place came to be known as Kashyapmar or the some other historians dispute that this valley was so called only when the people of Kash caste settled here permanently.

House Boats of Kashmir

The gentle sounds of rippling waters and the beautiful houseboats are the greatest attractions of Kashmir. Made up of cedar wood, these mesmerizing water boat residences have elegance and are complete with stately living quarters, drawing and dining rooms, carved wooden furniture, glowingly embroidered rugs and fabrics. The large windows of the houseboats provide beautiful views of the snow-covered peaks of the Himalayan Mountains and the pretty Dal Lake with beautiful lotus flowers adorning it. The breathtaking views combined with the silent and serene atmosphere and homely comforts are enough to infuse new lives and rejuvenate the visitors.

There are wide varieties of houseboats, one can choose from, according to one's needs and requirements. '*Firdaus*' are known for their grandeur and has three double bedrooms with attached bathrooms, hot and cold water and a lavish living room. '*Khushal*' is a little smaller with two double bedrooms along with the other desired comforts. However, the most beloved of the honeymooners are '*Nishat*' and '*Khushdil*' with one double bedroom, privacy and comforts along with the beautiful views of the lake. The Dal Lake or Nagin Lake of Srinagar is also famous for its '*Shikaras*', the floating vegetable gardens; the visitors love to have a ride on, to all the way to the Mughals' Paradise.

Besides the homely comforts and delicacies of the houseboat and the famous Shikara ride, the other luxuries one can enjoy are sunbathing on the houseboats on the top-deck. Water - powered peddlers sell everything from saffron to papier mache deer to the houseboat door.

JAMMU CITY

The city of Jammu, besides being the winter capital of the state, is also known as the city of temples. It is believed that Raja Jamboo Lochan originally founded the city in the 14th century. According to the popular legend, while the Raja was hunting one day, he happened to witness a tiger and a goat drinking water side by side from one and the same pond. He was so struck by this extraordinary phenomenon that he decided to build a city at this site so that the strong and weak could live together in peace and mutual tolerance. Eventually, he founded the city, which came to be known as "Jamboo" after his own name. The name later distorted to that of Jammu as it is called now.

In 1730, the city came under the rule of the Dogra king, Raja Dhruv Deva and under the patronage of Dogra rulers; Jammu became an important centre of art and culture, especially the Pahari School of paintings. Today, the beautiful city of Jammu boasts of innumerable temples and shrines, refreshing environs, pleasant climate, breathtaking views and harmonious existence of Hindus and Muslims.

Climate: Summers in Jammu are pleasant to warm with temperatures ranging from 23.4°C to 43°C while winter are chilly with temperature as low as 4.3°C. There is heavy snowfall in the winters too.

Jammu Temples

Situated in the foothills of the Himalayas, is the place that Raja Jambu Lochan discovered one day along the River Tawi, while he was on a hunting trip. To his surprise, he found that a tiger and a goat stood side-by-side, drinking water from the same place in the Tawi River. He was so struck by this unusual sight that he decided to build a city here where no living creature seemed to bear enmity towards each other. Today, as if in testimony to Raja Jambu Lochan's vision, the city of Jammu has come to be known as the 'City Of Temples'. Innumerable temples and shrines with 'shikhars' soaring into the sky create the ambience of a holy and peaceful city.

Amongst the temples in Jammu, the *Raghunath Mandir* takes pride of place being situated right in the heart of the city. This temple is situated at the city centre and was built in 1857. This temple consists of seven shrines, each with a tower of its own. It is the largest temple complex in northern India. Though 130 years old, the complex is remarkable for sacred scriptures, one of the richest collections of ancient texts and manuscripts in its library.

Its arches, surface and niches are undoubtedly influenced by Mughal architecture while the interiors of the temple are plated with gold. The main sanctuary is dedicated to Vishnu's eighth incarnation and Dogras' patron deity, the Rama. It also houses a Sanskrit Library containing rare Sanskrit manuscripts.

The famous temple of Bawey Wali Mata inside the Bahu Fort attracts pilgrims every Tuesday and Sunday who come here to worship the presiding deity of Jammu while opposite the Bahu Fort, overlooking the River Tawi is a temple dedicated to Mahamaya, a local heroine of Dogras, who lost her life fourteen centuries ago fighting foreign invaders.

The present temple of Bawey Wali Mata was built shortly after the coronation of Maharaja Gulab Singh, in 1822. It is also known as the temple of Mahakali and the goddess is considered second only to Mata Vaishno Devi in terms of mystical power.

Alongside the same river are the Peer Kho Cave temple, the Panchbakhtar temple and the Ranbireshwar temple dedicated to Lord Shiva with their own legends and specific days of worship. The Ranbireshwar Temple has twelve Shiva 'lingams' of crystal measuring 12" to 18" and galleries with thousands of 'saligrams' fixed on stone slabs.

The Dargah (shrine) of Peer Budhan Ali Shah or Peer Baba is said to protect the people of this city from mishaps and evil spirits. A friend of Guru Gobind Singh, it is said that Peer Baba lived his entire life on milk alone and lived to the age of five hundred and still people from all faiths and religions verate him in equal respect.

Peer Mitha was a saint who has a shrine of his own and was a contemporary of Ajaib Dev and Ghareeb Nath, who were famous for their prophecies and miracles. 'Mitha' means 'the sweet one' and the saint was so-called, as the Peer would accept nothing more than a pinch of sugar in offering from his devotees.

Worship of Shakti is prevalent in all parts of Jammu province and the best known of the Shakti shrines is the temple of Vaishno Devi, which holds the same status in Jammu as the Amarnath cave has in Kashmir. 61 km. north of Jammu, this cave temple is dedicated to Mahakali, Mahalaxmi and Mahasaraswati, the three mother goddesses of Hinduism. The cave is one of the region's most important pilgrim sites. There is a 13 km. track to the cave temple and the ponies, porters and dandies are available from Katra to cave temple in a fixed rate.

Jammu Museum: In the north, Jammu's two museums display a valuable collection of miniature paintings collectively known as 'Pahari' school of paintings or hill school of paintings. In Srinagar, there is a *Shri Pratap Singh (SPS) Museum*, which is the only place in India where one can see stone sculptures of deities executed in the distinctive style that was a hallmark of Kashmir in the 7th to 11th centuries. The two museums of Jammu are: -

Amar Mahal Palace Museum: A beautiful red sand stone palace, it stands amidst the most picturesque surroundings of Jammu. In the north are pretty Shivaliks along with the gorgeous gurgling River Tawi that adds grandeur to this already picture-perfect place. It was once the residential palace of Raja Amar Singh that has now been converted to a museum. Hari-Tara Charitable trust looks after the palace now. The highlight of the museum is the splendid golden throne, a 120 kg pure gold sofa, which is ornamented by the golden lions embedded into it. It is placed in a hexagonal room. There is a gallery in the museum that exhibit paintings known as Nal Damyanti along with other Pahari paintings and family portraits of rulers of Jammu and Kashmir. The museum also houses a library of around 25000 books on various subjects and disciplines. The building of the museum itself is a visual treat and is designed like a French Chateau.

Dogra Art Museum: Situated in the Pink Hall of Mubarak Mandi complex, the museum has on its display about 800 rare and exquisite paintings from different schools of paintings such as Basoli, Jammu and Kangra. It houses a gold plated bow and arrow belonging to Mughal Emperor Shah Jehan and a number of carpentry tools that are also an important section of the museum. There are hand written manuscripts of Shahnama and Sikendernama, written in Persian, housed here alon with a stone plate on which Takri script has been inscribed.

LEH CITY

Flying into Leh, the cold desert land, over the magnificent Himalayas is a beautiful and scary experience at once. Leh Palace illuminated by huge halogen lamps looks like a bewitching castle on a hilltop set ablaze in the dark nights of the Leh. Drive in the city is as exciting as the wonders it has in its lap with the long isolated winding road that opens up into a sheer expanse of arid flatness in burnt sienna. There is blinding sun at the top and perhaps at the first impression, a visitor is not likely to appreciate the blessings of the land fully.

Bon and Buddhism rule the lifestyle and culture of the people here. The Chortens (Stupas) and enchanting Gompas (Monasteries) adorn the city with their presence. The landscape is breathtakingly beautiful and there is an ominous beauty in the stark surroundings of Laddakh. The Hinayana Buddhist way of life lends a benevolent spirit to the very air of the region.

Climate: The days are dry and warm with cool winds blowing. The highest temperature is 25°C in summers and 10°C in winters while the nights are cool with temperatures ranging between 14°C and 8°C. There is heavy rainfall in winters. Recently, there has been increasing incidents of sporadic rainfall throughout the year.

Leh Palace: The captivating Leh Palace rises from the edge of a hill overlooking the town and at once looks like a reminiscent of Lhasa's Potala Palace. Though deserted, it has some definite mystical quality about it. The Palace was built in the middle of the 16th century by King Singe Namgyal and still belongs to the royal family that now lives in the Stok Palace. The nine-storeyed monument is now in ruins. The palace remains locked and may be opened at request by a monk.

The Palace has a museum with some tangkhas (painted or embroidered scrolls) and paintings on its display. The view from the monastery above the Leh Palace is quite impressive. It is known as Namgyal Tsemo Gompa (monastery). The red monastery has some frescos, Buddhist scriptures, idols and a massive statue of the Maitreya Buddha (future Buddha).

The striking Shanti Stupa is a recent structure. Japanese, who harbored the ambition of spreading Buddhism across the world, had it constructed in 1985 with aid from the Japanese Government. A motorable road and a steep flight of stairs connect the Stupa to the town, where one can relax and enjoy the panoramic view of the chain of mountains and the peaceful little village of Changspa with typical Laddakhi houses. The stream flowing near the village and the towering Namgyal Tsemo in the distance, are also visible from here.

TOURISM IN JAMMU AND KASHMIR

Jammu and Kashmir is the northernmost state of India locked in Himalayan Mountains. Jammu and Kashmir is home to several Valleys such as the Kashmir Valley, Tawi, Chenab Valley, Poonch, Sindh Valley and Lidder Valley. Some major tourist attractions in Jammu and Kashmirare Srinagar, the Mughal Gardens, Gulmarg, Pahalgam, Patnitop, Jammu, and Ladakh. Some areas require a special permit for non-Indiansto visit.

Gulmarg Gondola, Cable Car

Regions

The Vaishno Devi shrine attracts millions of Hindu devotees every year, located in Jammu region.

Shikaras on Dal Lake in Kashmir region.

The 9 Stupas at Thiksey Monastery

- Jammu — Jammu is the winter capital of state and known for its temples, particularly The Vaishno Devi Temple in Katra which is visited by over 1 crore (10 million) pilgrims every year, making Jammu the most visited part of Jammu and Kashmir State.

- Kashmir Valley — is visited for its gardens, lakes, and pristine streams and landscapes. Kashmir Valley consists of many ancient temples and shrines which makes it an important site for Hindus and Buddhists.
- Ladakh — consists rivers like Indus river. The peaks in the Ladakh Range are at a medium altitude close to the Zoji-la (5,000–5,500 m or 16,000–18,050 ft) and increase toward the southeast, culminating in the twin summits of Nun-Kun (7000 m or 23,000 ft).

Tourist Attractions

- Jammu — the winter capital
- Srinagar — the summer capital of the state, set around Dal Lake, with its floating houseboats
- Gulmarg — Skiing and the India' highest gondola
- Katra— in the foothills of the Trikuta Mountains and home of the holy Mata Vaishno Devi shrine
- Leh — the jumping off point for treks and adventures around Ladakh
- Pahalgam — a calm and serene place offering multiple trekking routes. Starting point of Amarnath Yatra
- Patnitop — a small hill station in Jammu
- Kishtwar locked between Himalayas and known for Saffron.

Overview

Before militancy intensified in 1989, tourism formed an important part of the Kashmiri economy and Kashmir was the favorite destination for Bollywood. Kashmir had 19 cinema halls which were closed due to rising Islamic Terrorism. The tourism economy in the Kashmir valley was worst hit. However, the holy shrines of Jammu and the Buddhist monasteries of Ladakh continue to remain popular pilgrimage and tourism destinations. Every year, thousands of Hindu pilgrims visit holy shrines of Vaishno Devi and Amarnath which has had significant impact on the state's economy.

Tourism in the Kashmir valley has rebounded in recent years and in 2009, the state became one of the top tourist destinations of India.Gulmarg, one of the most popular ski resort destinations in India, is also home to the world's highest green golf course. The decrease in violence in the state has boosted the states economy specifically tourism. It was reported that 7.36 lakh tourists visited Kashmir in 2010 including 23,000 foreigners. In 2011, the number of tourist arrivals in Kashmir touched the mark of 10 lakh.

Language

The state's official language is Urdu. However, the main languages spoken are Kashmiri in the Kashmir Valley, Ladakhi in Ladakh and Dogri in Jammu. Most people can speak Hindias a second language.

As elsewhere in India, English is fairly widely spoken among the educated classes and those involved in the tourist industry.

Transportation

By plane

Srinagar International Airport

Flights operate to Jammu, Leh and Srinagar. Air India, Jet Airways, Air Asia, GoAir, Indigo Airlines and SpiceJet are some of the flights operating in the state.

By train

Banihal Railway station.

The last stop on the railway line north is Shri Mata Vaishno Devi Katra railway station, where you can catch onward buses and hire SUVs/MUVs (Tata Sumo / Toyota Innova/ Mahindra Scorpio).

However it is better to get down in Jammu and catch a taxi from there as these are more readily available.

The Jammu–Baramulla line is a railway line being built in India to connect the state of Jammu and Kashmir with the rest of the country.

The Project officially coded USBRL (Udhampur Srinagar Baramulla Railway Link) starts from the city of Udhampur, 55 kilometres (34 mi) north of Jammu, and travels for 290 kilometres (180 mi) to the city of Baramulla on the northwestern edge of the Kashmir Valley.

The route crosses major earthquake zones, and is subjected to extreme temperatures of cold and heat, as well as inhospitable terrain, making it an extremely challenging engineering project.

By Bus

There are two ways to get in by land - via Jammu and up to Srinagar or via Manali in Himachal Pradesh and up to Leh.

Transportation within

Sanji Chhat helipad vaishno devi

- Buses are operated by J&K SRTC to most points around the state. They offer package tour to Gulmarg, Shonmarg, Yusmarg, Wular lake, City tour, etc. There is Tourist information center, where one get the tickets plus info.
- 4 wheel drive jeeps are quicker, a little more expensive and reach more locations. Private hire jeeps are also available.

Tourist places

Gulmarg

Gulmarg is well known for its natural environment and it is counted as one of unique tourist destinations in the India. Gulmarg is surrounded by dense forest. This place has a highland golf course. There is a special Gondola ride(ropeway) from Gulmarg.

Vaishno Devi

The town of Katra, which is close to Jammu, contains the Vaishno Devi shrine. Nestling on top of the Trikuta Hills at a height of 1700 m is the sacred cave shrine of Vaishno Devi, the mother goddess. At a distance of 48 km from Jammu, the cave is 30 metres long and just 1.5 metres high. At the end of the cave are shrines dedicated to the three forms of the mother goddess — Mahakali, Mahalakshmi and Mahasarasvati, which is manifested as Vaishno Devi. Pilgrims start trekking to the cave temple, which is 13 km from Katra, enter in small groups through a narrow opening and walk through ice waters to reach the shrines.

Sonmarg

Sonmarg Valley

The way to reach Sonmarg or the Meadow of the gold is from the Sindh Valley. This valley also shows more amazing facet in Kashmir. Sonmarg is located at an altitude of around 2730 meters from the sea level; it has snow-covered mountains as its backdrop against the sky. The ZOZILLA path which is one of the deadliest roads on the earth can be travelled from here.

Raghunath Temple

Raghunath Temple is dedicated to the Hindu Lord Shri Rama. All the inner walls of this temple are covered with gold, on three sides. Galleries of this temples are covered with ' Saligrams'. The other surrounding temples are related to other gods from the Ramayana. This temple is located in the centre or we can say in the heart of Jammu.

Mubarak Mandi Palace

Mubarak Palace was built with the touch of three different styles, Rajasthani, Mughal and Gothic. Most famous part of this Palace is the Sheesh Mahal segment. There is a Dogra Art Museum, which is a treasure house of miniature paintings from various hill schools.

In Kashmir Valley

- Vernag Spring and Mughal Garden- A fresh water spring and a Mughal garden next to it, spring is chief source of Jhelum River.
- Amarnath temple - pilgrimage site for Hindu devotees of Shiva.
- Srinagar - Summer Capital of Jammu and Kashmir, a popular hill station
- Dal lake - a lake in Srinagar, with house boats called shikharas.
- Manasbal Lake
- Shalimar Gardens—Mughal Garden
- Nishant Gardens-Mughal Garden
- Chashme Shahi- Mughal Garden

- Pari Mahal- old monument of Pari Mahal, one can have full view of Dal Lake.
- Shankaracharya Temple- Ancient Temple of Lord Shiva

Skiing is popular in Gulmarg, showing cable car in a snow clad mountain.

Shikara In A Row

- Hari Parbat- Ancient Temple of Goddess Sharika Bhagwati and an old fort on this hill.
- Kheer Bhawani Temple

- Martand Sun Temple - a Kashmiri Hindu temple dedicated to Surya (the chief solar deity in Hinduism) and built during the 8th century CE. *Martand* is another Sanskrit name for the Hindu Sun-god. Now in ruins, the temple is located five miles from Anantnag.
- Gulmarg - Popular hill station and skiing destination.
- Pahalgam - Hill station
- Betaab Valley- A lush green valley 06 km from Pahalgam where the movie Betaab was shot.
- Sonmarg - Hill station
- Yusmarg - Hill station
- Aru - scenic valley
- Lolab Valley - Least disturbed camping site and lush green valley
- Eco-tourism places:Gurez, Bangus Valley.

In Jammu

Paragliding in Sanasar

The Vaishno Devi shrine

- Vaishno Devi - Hindu shrine.
- Patnitop - Hill station
- Bhaderwah - Hill station
- Poonch
- Sanasar
- Eco-tourism places: Mantalai and Shivkhori
- Bhimgarh Fort
- Ramnagar Fort in Udhampur District
- Mansar Lake with its length more than a mile and width half-a-mile, is a very attractive lake in the midst of lusting greeneries surrounded by forest-covered hills. It is considered as a very holy site known from mythological periods sharing the sanctity and legacy of Mansa Sarovar. It is a very popular base of tourists.

In Ladakh

- Leh - One of the two districts of Ladakh, with monasteries.
- Nubra Valley - the scenic valley with towns of Deskit and Hundar.
- Lake Moriri - one of the largest and high altitude lakes.
- Pangong Lake - Lake divided between India and China
- Zanskar - scenic trekking areas.
- Suru Valley - Origin of various glaciers, Nun and Kun Peaks
- Drass - World's Second Coldest Inhabited Place, site of the 1999 Kargil war. Must visit Dras War Memorial

8

Population and Religion

POPULATION OF JAMMU AND KASHMIR 2018

Jammu and Kashmir is a state situated in north India, as often indicated by the acronym J&K. It is located for the most part in the Himalayan Mountains and has its borders with Himachal Pradesh and Punjab. It also has an international border with China in the north and east, the Line of Control isolated it from the Pakistani areas of Azad Kashmir in the west. It has a one of a kind autonomy under Article 370 of the Constitution of India.

A piece of the territory of Kashmir and Jammu, the region is the subject of a conflict among China, India and Pakistan. The western areas of the past regal state known as Azad Kashmir and Gilgit-Baltistan have been under Pakistani control since 1947. The Aksai Chin range bordering Tibet has been under the control of China since 1962.

The state has been an indispensable area for some Bollywood movies and one of them is Rockstar. Jammu and Kashmir has its very own appeal and draws in many people from everywhere throughout the nation.

Population Of Jammu And Kashmir In 2018

According to the 2011 evaluation, the number of inhabitants in the state was 12,548,925 and it is the lone state with a larger population of Muslims. Talking about population, in order to check out the population of Jammu & Kashmir in 2018, we need to have a look at the population of the past 5 years. They are as per the following:

1. 2013 – 13.1 Million
2. 2014 – 13.3 Million
3. 2015 – 13.6 Million
4. 2016 – 13.9 Million
5. 2017 – 14.12 Million

Predicting the 2018 population of Jammu & Kashmir is not easy but we can get the idea after analysing the population from the year 2013 – 17. As we have seen that every year the population increases by 0.204 Million. Hence, the population of Jammu & Kashmir in 2018 is forecast to be 14.12 Million + 0.204 Million = 14.324 Million. So, the population of Jammu & Kashmir in the year 2018 as per estimated data = 14.324 Million.

Jammu & Kashmir Population 2018 –14.324 Million. (estimated).

Demography Of Jammu And Kashmir

Jammu and Kashmir is the solitary Indian state with a more prominent Muslim population. According to the 2011 list, Islam is followed by around 68.3% of the population, while 28.4% belong to Hinduism, Sikhism (1.7%), Buddhism (0.7%) and Christians (0.5%). Around 96.4% of the people in the Kashmir valley is Muslim, trailed by Hindus and Sikhs. Shia population out here is 15 Lakhs in Jammu and Kashmir, which is 14% of entire state population.

Population Density And Growth Of Jammu And Kashmir

The population density of the state is 56 persons per square kilometre. It has contained its population growth by around 6% in the decade from 2001 to 2011, as showed by figures released by state Directorate of Census Operations. From 29.43% out in 2001, the population growth of Jammu & Kashmir has declined to 23.64% in 2011.

Facts About Jammu And Kashmir:

1. It has an International Border with China and in addition Line of Control (LOC) separates Jammu and Kashmir from Pakistan.
2. Jammu City is hot in the midst of summer and the temperature touches upto 40 degree Celsius. The Ladakh region is to a great degree cold.
3. The perfect circumstances to visit this state are April to October and in addition December to January.
4. There are around 22 regions out here in Jammu and Kashmir.
5. Jammu is the Winter Capital and Srinagar is basically the Summer Capital. Srinagar is the Largest City of Jammu & Kashmir.

DEMOGRAPHICS

Religion in Jammu And Kashmir (2011)

Islam (68.31%)

Hinduism (28.43%)

Sikhism (1.87%)

Buddhism (0.89%)

Christianity (0.28%)

Jainism (0.01%)

Other or none (0.01%)

Atheist (0.001%)

Languages of Jammu and Kashmir (2011)

Kashmiri (53.27%)

Hindi (20.83%)

Dogri (20.04%)

Punjabi (1.75%)

Other (4.11%)

The major ethnic groups living in Jammu and Kashmir include Kashmiris, Gujjars/Bakarwals, Paharis, Dogras and Ladakhis. The Kashmiris live mostly in the main valley of Kashmir and Chenab valley of Jammu division with a minority living in the Pir Panjal region. The Pahari-speaking people mostly live in and around the Pir Panjal region with some in the northern Kashmir valley. The nomadic Gujjars and Bakerwals practice transhumance and mostly live in the Pirpanjal region. The Dogras are ethnically, linguistically and culturally related to the neighboring Punjabi people and mostly live in the Udhampur and Jammu districts of the state. The Ladakhis inhabit Ladakh region.

Jammu and Kashmir is one of India's two administrative divisions (the other being the Union territory of Lakshadweep which is overwhelmingly Muslim) with a Muslim majority population. According to the 2011 census, Islam is practised by about 68.3% of the state population, while 28.4% follow Hinduism and small minorities follow Sikhism (1.9%), Buddhism (0.9%) and Christianity (0.3%). About 96.4% of the population of the Kashmir valley are Muslim followed by Hindus (2.45%) and Sikhs (0.98%) and others (0.17%) Shias live in the district of Badgam, where they are a majority. The Shia population is estimated to comprise 14% of the state's population.

In Jammu, Hindus constitute 62.55% of the population, Muslims 33.45% and Sikhs, 3.3%; In Ladakh (comprises Buddhists-dominated Leh and Shia Muslim-dominated Kargil), Muslims constitute about 46.4% of the population, the remaining being Buddhists (39.7%) and Hindus (12.1%).The people of Ladakh are of Indo-Tibetan origin, while the southern area of Jammu includes many communities tracing their ancestry to the nearby Indian states of Haryana and Punjab, as well as the city of Delhi.

According to political scientist Alexander Evans, approximately 99% of the total population of 160,000–170,000 of Kashmiri Brahmins, also called Kashmiri Pandits, (*i.e.* approximately 150,000 to 160,000) left the Kashmir Valley in

1990 as militancy engulfed the state. According to an estimate by the Central Intelligence Agency, about 300,000 Kashmiri Pandits from the entire state of Jammu and Kashmir have been internally displaced due to the ongoing violence.

The pre-independence Census of 1941 recorded Muslims as constituting 72.41% of the population, and Hindus 25.01%. In the 1961 census, the first one to be conducted after the partition of the State, Muslims constituted 68.31% of the population and Hindus 28.45%. The proportion of Muslims fell to 64.19% by 1981 but recovered afterward, reaching 68.31% again by 2011.

In Jammu and Kashmir, the principal spoken languages are Kashmiri, Urdu, Dogri, Hindi, Punjabi, Pahari, Balti, Ladakhi, Gojri, Shina and Pashto. However, Urdu written in the Persian script is the official language of the state. Hindustani is widely understood by peoples. Many speakers of these languages use Urdu or English as a second language.

Urdu occupies a central space in media, education, religious and political discourses, and the legislature of Jammu and Kashmir. The language is said to function as a symbol of identity among Muslims of South Asia. Additionally, as the language is regarded as a "neutral" and non-native language of the multilingual region, its acceptance was broadly accepted by Kashmiri Muslims. The use of Urdu as the official language of Jammu and Kashmir has also been criticised by Rajeshwari V. Pandharipande of the University of Illinois on the basis that the language is spoken as a native language by less than 1% of the population, and has rendered Kashmiri, spoken by 53% of the population, into a functional "minority language," effectively restricting its use to home and family.

The Kashmir Valley is dominated by ethnic Kashmiris, who have largely driven the campaign for secession from India. Non-Kashmiri Muslim ethnic groups (Paharis, Gujjars and Bakarwalas), who dominate areas along the Line of Control, have remained indifferent to the separatist campaign. Jammu province region has a 70:30 Hindu-Muslim ratio. Parts of the region were hit by militants, but violence has ebbed there, along with the Valley, after India and Pakistan started a peace process in 2004.

Dogras (67%) are the single largest group in the multi-ethnic region of Jammu living with Punjabis, Kashmiris, Paharis, Bakerwals and Gujjars. Statehood is demanded in Hindu-dominated districts. Ladakh is the largest region in the state with over 200,000 people. Its two districts are Leh (68% Buddhist) and Kargil (91% Muslim population). Union territory status has been the key demand of Leh Buddhists for many years.

PEOPLE OF KASHMIR

The people of Kashmir are believed to be the descendants of the immigrants from India proper. As Buddhism spread here, people from far and wide came for research and study. People of Kashmir experience a culture that is an amalgamation of a number of other cultures they came in contact with. Roman, Greek and Persian civilizations have influenced the culture of Kashmiri people to quite an extent. Kashmiri population is a blend of people belonging to distinct races with different looks, dresses, food habits, customs, traditions, rituals, etc. Have a look at the people and main ethnic groups in Jammu and Kashmir.

Kashmiri Pandits

Kashmiri Pandits are amongst the original inhabitants of the valley. They used to dominate the region of Kashmir, at one point of time. However, acute terrorism in the Kashmir valley forced them to migrate to other places in the country. Today, their population has been reduced to minority in Kashmir.

Kashmiri Muslims

Approximately ninety percent of the population of Kashmir consists of Kashmiri Muslims. Muslims belonging to both the Shia sect and the Sunni sect reside in the valley. They are considered to be quite skillful in arts and crafts. Their other occupations include agriculture, sheep rearing, cattle rearing and other cottage industries.

Gujjars

Gujjars are considered to be the Rajasthani Rajputs, who converted to Muslim faith. They belong to the hilly area of Kashmir and are generally herdsmen by occupation. Tall and well built, Gujjars have notably Jewish features.

Kashmiri women love to dress up with a lot of ornaments. Almost every body part, be it the head, ears, neck, arms or ankles, is adorned with jewelry. A typical ornament of a married Kashmiri Pandit woman is Dejharoo. It is a pair of gold pendants, which hangs on a silk thread or gold chain and passes through holes in the ears pieced at the top end of the lobes. The Muslim women are quite fond of wearing a bunch of earrings. The typical dress of a Kashmiris man is Pheran, a long loose gown hanging down below the knees. The men wear a skullcap, a close-fitting shalwar (Muslims) or churidar pyjama (Pandits) and lace less shoes called gurgabi. In case of Kashmiri women, the Pheran is either knee-length (Muslim) or touching the feet (Hindu). The Pheran is tied at the waist with folded material called lhungi.

RELIGIONS IN KASHMIR

Three major faiths are clearly dominant in different parts of Jammu and Kashmir. However, in terms of total population, Islam clearly dominates the Kashmir valley. You will find the valley brimming with Muslim population. In addition to that Hinduism and Buddhism also constitute a part of the religions in Kashmir. The followers of Buddhism inhabit the Ladakh area of Jammu and Kashmir State.

Islam

The predominant religion of Kashmir valley is Islam. Muslims constitute more than 90% of the total population of Jammu and Kashmir. Even in Jammu, Kargil and some other districts, Islam forms a substantial part of the population. The Muslims are broadly divided into two sects - the Sunnis and the Shias.

Hinduism

Hinduism is the second most dominant faith in Kashmir. The majority of Hindus consist of Kashmiri Pandits and Gujjars. Majority of the Kashmiri Pandits migrated from the Kashmir valley because of the constant terror threat and are now present in a minority. On the other hand, many Gujjars got converted to Islam.

Buddhism

Buddhist population is mainly found in the Ladakh region of Kashmir, where it predominates. In the main Kashmir valley, however, Buddhists are present in a negligible numbers.

9

Art, Architecture, Fair and Festivals

ARTS AND CRAFT OF JAMMU AND KASHMIR

The splendid work of art and craft in Jammu and Kashmir makes it famous all over the world. Some kind of elegant art work is present almost in everything in Jammu and Kashmir, be it embroidery on the shawls, papier-mache and steel ware and wood work.

The villages of Anantnag and Srinagar have been quite famous for enhancing the beauty of arts and craft of Jammu and Kashmir. They are world famous for carpets and wooden furniture. Along with it, the antique items include Shahtoosh Shawls and Pashmina shawls. Crewel ware, brass and silver ware are other interesting articles.

Following are the famous art and crafts of Jammu and Kashmir:

Carpets

Definitely, one of the most expensive and world renowned arts of Kashmir. Originally, the art of making carpets started from Samarkand in Central Asia. Later, the process itself witnessed a tremendous growth with the artisans from Iran experimenting with the motifs and textures. Carpets from Kashmir are made of wool and even silk, are available in a large number of variety.

Basket weaving

These are made of willow rushes and this form of weaving can be used to make baskets or even lamp-shades. A little expensive, they can also be used as glass holders or picnic baskets. Hazratbal in Srinagar is known for basket weaving throughout India.

Embroidery

The typical Kashmiri embroidery is known as Kasida and is famous all over the world. It is very exquisite in its execution and is very rich and elaborate in colour. Quite interestingly, this embroidery, which is often done on saris and shawls, does not have a wrong side to it.

Pashmina Shawls

The fleecy wool obtained from the Kel goat is used for making the Pashmina Shawls in Kashmir. They are very famous, even at the international levels, and are locally called as 'ring shawls.'

This is because they are so delicate and elegant, that they can easily pass from a ring, itself. A high value and elegant shawl has designs and motifs, equally embellished on both the sides.

Papier Mache

No matter how similar the papier mache articles look at the first glance, they have their own differences and originality. Three grades of paper are used for its designing. In the process of making it, paper is soaked in water till the time it disintegrates. Then an adhesive solution is used to mix it over, eventually moulding it into different shapes which are later coloured and varnished.

Tweed

Pure wool is used to for weaving it. It is one of the highly exported articles in arts and crafts of Jammu and Kashmir. This silk weaving further enhances the beauty of sericulture in Kashmir. Over the years, it has been aflourishing form of art and crafts in Kashmir.

So, why wait? If you are an art connoisseur, just delve into exploring the richness of the arts and handicrafts of Jammu and Kashmir with our special packages.

ARTS AND CRAFTS TOURISM

Papier Mache Work, Kashmir

Art and Crafts of Jammu and Kashmir - Magic without Illusions

The state of Jammu and Kashmir is famous the world over for its unique and splendid work of art and crafts. Travel through even the remotest parts of the state will give an insight into the world of art and craft in Jammu and Kashmir. Just about everything that is seen in Jammu and Kashmir has some kind of art work done on it. The most prominent is the embroidery work on the shawls and the cloths of Kashmiri people are very mesmerizing to be not noticed. You will also see the work of magic in wood works, steel wares, Papier-mache.

Textile Works

Shawls are the most famous offering of textile works from Jammu and Kashmir. The final product is definitely impressive, but the method by which they are produced is equally interesting.

Even in the era of power looms, people of the state prefer making their textiles the traditional way. The shawls are made of a special wool, called the Pashmina that is extracted from the Kel goat.

The shawls are then formed in two ways. In one way the weaving is done on the loom itself and in other, the embroidery is done by hand after looming. The embroidery that is done in J&K is called Kasida. In embroidery, use of exquisite colored threads is done to make designs of Chinar leaves, mythological figures or landscape designs. J&K also have become famous for its silk quality and quantity. In fact silk products are exported from J&K in huge amount. Main clothes that are made of silk are sarees, ladies suits and head coverings.

Papier Mache

Papier Mache is another form of handicraft that has brought J&K wide acclaim from all regions of the world. To make Papier Mache objects, the process is very long and tedious. First the paper is soaked in water till the time it completely dismantles. The paper is then mashed and is mixed with an adhesive solution. The pulp is then molded into desired shape and is dried. The outlay of the object is now ready. Now is the time for artisans to color it and draw intricate and brilliant designs on it. The product is now ready to hit the market. The first look on these splendorous object itself will compel you to make them your own. There are cheaper versions of Papier Mache as well that are made up of cardboard. Pen boxes, table lamps, show pieces and other decorative items are few that are made from Papier Mache.

Wood Carvings

Wood Carving industry has grown by leaps and bounds in the last few years in J&K. In fact, wood carving industry of J&K is the most famous in entire country. The Walnut wood is considered the best wood for carvings. Not only because it is readily available, but even after excessive carvings, the wood retains its strength.

The main attraction of woodcarvings is the woodwork on the ceiling of the rooms. The technique for this work is immensely complicated and the end product is equally mesmerizing. This kind of woodcarving is called Khatam Band. Woodcarving can also be seen on chairs, tables, jewelry boxes and on any thing and every thing that is made of woods.

Art and craft is something that you will see, touches every aspect of life in J&K. Be it the clothes they wear or the homes they live in, everything in some way or the other has crafts involved in it. Most of these things are brilliant enough to be taken home as souvenirs of your travel to J&K. Lal Chowk and Badshah Chowk in Srinagar and Vir Marg and Hari Market is Jammu are the best places where you can indulge in shopping.

ARCHITECTURE OF JAMMU AND KASHMIR

Architecture of Jammu and Kashmir comprises architecture of Srinagar, Kashmir, Jammu and Ladakh which are different from each other. Over all the architecture of Jammu and Kashmir is an interesting combination of holy shrines, mosques, gardens and museums. There is a curious intermingling of both Islamic, Buddhist and Hindu architecture in Jammu and Kashmir. The architectures of Jammu and Kashmir bear the splendour of the kingdoms that have ruled the valley. There has been an amalgamation of culture in Jammu and Kashmir. The architectural skill of the Mughals and the elaborate detailing of the Hindu architecture have all contributed to the awe inspiring nature of Jammu and Kashmir architecture. Under emperor

Ashoka, Kashmir also flourished under the impact of Buddhist culture.

Amar Mahal Palace

In Jammu and Kashmir there is blend of several cultures which have had an impact on its architecture. During the 3rd century BC when Emperor Ashokareigned over India, Kashmir came under his rule and Buddhist culture flourished. During the 4th century, BC, Alexander brought along the Hellenic culture. Perhaps Hellenic culture also influenced the architecture of the era, but no buildings of that period remain. A glimpse of it can be seen in temples built during the Hindu era, especially in the corridors surrounding the Hindu temples of Buniyar and Martand. Hindu architecture of Jammu and Kashmir was marked by the stone structures. During the fourteenth century, Islam spread and mosques were being built all over.

The mosques were made of wood with a steeple covering them, instead of a dome. This wooded mosque is an exclusive architecture of Jammu and Kashmir and only few are found in Kerala. This is because Muslims adopted the traditional architectural style used for Hindu temples even though they changed the building material. Another characteristic feature of that era is the gardens, built in 1586, by Emperor Akbar when he ruled over Kashmir and visited it every summer.

The temples, mosques and gardens of Jammu and Kashmir are mostly centered in Srinagar. The Mughal gardens like the Shalimar garden, Nishatbagh, Nila Nag bagh and the Begamabad bagh are all architectures of Srinagar.

Apart from the picturesque garden the phase of the classical architecture of Kashmir is represented by the Brahmanical buildings dating from the eighth to the thirteenth century A.D. Of these structures the most impressive is certainly the sun-temple at Martand, which appears to have served as a model for all later Brahmanical shrines.

It was built by King Lalitaditya in the middle of the eighth century A.D. The Vishnu temple of Buniar is another example of Hindu temple architecture.

Islamic architecture of Srinagar is perceived in the Jami Masjid Friday mosque of Srinagar. The Jami Masjid is the most magnificent and fascinating of all wooden mosques in Kashmir. The architectural style of this mosque is adopted from the Hindu temples of Kashmir. In Jammuthe Amar Mahal palace is a fascinating piece of architecture. The structure of the palace is irregular in plan, it has gabled roofs, projecting in many directions and a colonnade made of wood, on the first floor.

Rizong Monastery

Ladakh in Jammu and Kashmir, on the other hand, is noteworthy for its monasteries. Buddhism had a strong influence in this region. The Lamayuru monastery stands on bleak, rocky mountain cape, very typical of Ladakh.

The multi storied structure with various spaces like temples, assembly halls and cells for the monks, is precariously perched on the steep slope. The fairly light buildings are built with a wooden framework, earthen walls and willow for floors. The Rizong monastery and the Themisgang monastery are the other Buddhist architecture. Cave temples are also a principal architecture of Ladakh in Jammu and Kashmir. In Leh there are some monasteries and palaces which enhance the architectural richness of Jammu and Kashmir.Architecture in Jammu and Kashmir is thus an amalgamation of Hindu, Islamic and Buddhist style of architecture. The Hindu temples, the Buddhist monasteries and the Mughal gardens make Jammu and Kashmir one of the most coveted destination on the world map.

FAIRS AND FESTIVALS IN JAMMU AND KASHMIR

The paradise on earth, Jammu and Kashmir is home to a rich cultural heritage, besides a panoramic landscape that leaves many a visitor spellbound. This culture and tradition is reflected in the several fairs and festivals in Jammu and Kashmir that are widely celebrated across the state with much zeal and gaiety. We at Indian Holiday take you on tours to Jammu and Kashmir that provide you with an exclusive opportunity to be a part of these memorable celebrations.

Almost all the major Hindu festivals in India are celebrated with equal enthusiasm in the state of Jammu and Kashmir. Some of such prominent fairs and festivals in Jammu and Kashmir include Lohri, Holi, Navratri, Baisakhi or New Year Day, Guru Ravi Das's Birthday, Tihar and Samkrant. People from across Jammu and Kashmir gather in large numbers during the time of these festivals. Interestingly, all Hindu,

Muslim or Sikh fairs and festivals are religiously observed in the entire state of Jammu and Kashmir. Besides the above, there are a number of other local fairs and festivals in Jammu and Kashmir that are celebrated with much fervor across the state. A large number of such festivals in Kashmir are associated with religious occasions and involve worship of deities. Besides these, J&K fairs in India are also a veritable reflection of the glorious culture and legacy of the state.

FAIRS AND FESTIVALS OF KASHMIR

Fairs and festivals of Jammu and Kashmir are a reflection of the diverse cultural and social heritage of the valley. Like all other parts of India, Kashmir too abounds with numerous fairs and festivals throughout the year. Fairs and festivals of Kashmir are celebrated with much fanfare and joy, regardless of the religion. Lohri is celebrated with as much enthusiasm as Id or Diwali. Given below is a list of the major fairs and festivals of Kashmir:

Lohri

The festival of Lohri is also celebrated as Makar Sakranti. It is celebrated on 13th January to welcome the onset of spring.

Baisakhi

Celebrated on 13th April, Baisakhi is the harvest festival of north India. It is also the day when Guru Gobind Singh founded the Khalsa sect.

Jhiri Mela

This fair is held to commemorate a poor farmer. It is believed that he committed suicide as protest against his tyrant landlord.

Purmandal Mela

This three-day fair is organized to commemorate the marriage of Lord Shiva and Goddess Parvati on Shivratri.

Bahu Mela

Bahu Mela is organized twice a year at the Kali temple in Bahu Fort of Jammu.

Mansar Food and Craft

Mela Mansar Food and Craft Mela is a three-day fair organized during Baisakhi season on the banks of the Mansar Lake.

Chaitre Chaudash

Chaitre Chaudash is held in the month of March-April at the village Uttar Behni.

Navratri

At the time of Navratri, a special mela (fair) is held at the Kheer Bhawani temple in the Tullamula village.

Eid-ul-Zoha

Eid-ul-Zoha is celebrated in the month of in July. It commemorates Prophet Abraham, who agreed to sacrifice his son to God.

Eid-ul-Fitr

Eid-ul-Fitr is celebrated in the month of October/November. It marks the end of the fasting month of Ramadan. On this occasion, sweets are prepared and Muslims buy new clothes and pamper themselves with delicious feasts.

10

Education

INTRODUCTION

Admin Block at Old University Campus, Government College of Engineering and Technology, Jammu

In 1970, the state government of Jammu and Kashmir established its own education board and university. Education in the state is divided into primary, middle, high secondary, college and university level. Jammu and Kashmir follows the 10+2 pattern for education of children. This is handled by Jammu and Kashmir State Board of School Education (abbreviated as JKBOSE). Private and public schools are recognized by the board to impart education to students. Board examinations are conducted for students in class VIII, X and XII. In addition, there are *Kendriya Vidyalayas* (run by the Government of India) and Indian Army schools that impart secondary school education. These schools follow the Central Board of Secondary Education pattern.

Notable higher education or research institutes in Jammu and Kashmir include the Indian Institute of Technology Jammu, Indian Institute of Management Jammu, National Institute of Technology, Srinagar, All India Institute of Medical Sciences, Jammu, Sher-i-Kashmir Institute of Medical Sciences, Srinagar, Government College of Engineering and Technology, Jammu, Government Medical College, Srinagar, All India Institute of Medical Science Awantipora , Acharya Shri Chandra college of medical sciences, Jammu and Government Medical College, Jammu, University-level education is provided by University of Kashmir, University of Jammu, Sher-e-Kashmir University of Agricultural Sciences and Technology, Srinagar, Sher-e-Kashmir University of Agricultural Sciences and Technology, Jammu, Islamic University of Science & Technology, Baba Ghulam Shah Badhshah University, Shri Mata Vaishno Devi University, Institution of Technicians and Engineers (Kashmir), Islamia College of Science and Commerce, Srinagar, Central University of Kashmir located at Ganderbal and Central University of Jammu located at Raya Suchani in the Samba district of Jammu.

EDUCATION IN JAMMU AND KASHMIR

The tourism industry of Jammu and Kashmir has made progress by leaps and bounds. But the same cannot be said for the education sector in the North Indian state. People from all over the world flock to Jammu and Kashmir to enjoy the state's natural beauty, but the poor educational set up here discourages students from traveling to Jammu and Kashmir to seek admission in its schools and colleges. Jammu and Kashmir had once been the center of learning for the Persian and Sanskrit languages during the start of the Indo – Aryan civilization. Gradually, the number of militant activities in the state increased and the political disturbances became a daily affair. These factors acted as barriers in the path of growth of education in Jammu and Kashmir. Over the past few years though the state government has been trying to revive the education situation in Jammu and Kashmir and inspiring more and more people to stay in the state for higher studies. In the last census report taken in the year 2009, Jammu and Kashmir had an impressive literacy rate of 59%. The literacy ratio of Kashmiri men and women stand a ratio of 65.75 : 41.82 percent.

Education System in Jammu and Kashmir

The political situation in Jammu and Kashmir is not very conducive to development of education or any other form of industry asides tourism. But nevertheless, the Central and the State government authorities have tried their best to promote academics here. Free education is provided to students who come from poor families and cannot pay the fee for even primary education. The education system in Jammu and Kashmir is divided into the respective tiers:

- Pre-Primary School
- Primary School
- Middle School
- High Secondary School
- College
- University

The Jammu and Kashmir education scenario has improved with time and the current student strength in this North Indian state stands at 1.5 million according to the 2009 census reports.

Primary Education in Jammu and Kashmir

The Jammu and Kashmir education board was established in the year 1970. There are more than 15000 schools within the state's boundaries today. Hindi is the medium of instruction for school education in Jammu and Kashmir. Schools have also been set up in the remote villages of the state, thereby giving a boost to rural education in Jammu and Kashmir. 2000 schools of Jammu and Kashmir are built in the rural areas and the state government authorities are trying to increase the number in order to eradicate illiteracy. Like in other parts of the country, Jammu and Kashmir also follows the 10+2 pattern of schooling. The schools in the North Indian state are affiliated to the Jammu and Kashmir State Board of School education (JKBOSE). In addition there is the Central Board of Secondary Education (CBSE) adopted by the Kendriya Vidyalayas and the Indian Army schools in the state. In Jammu and Kashmir, you have to give board examinations in class VIII, class X and class XII in order to pass the school level of education. Some well known schools in Jammu and Kashmir are:

Schools in Jammu and Kashmir

Sports and extra curricular activities are always encouraged in all Jammu and Kashmir schools. There are public schools in Jammu and Kashmir which exclusively provide education to the underprivileged and the Tibetan refugees. On the other hand there are private schools that cater to children of the elite.

Graduation and PG Level Courses in Jammu and Kashmir

There are many institutes of repute in Jammu and Kashmir that provide graduation and PG level courses to students. The Jammu and Kashmir colleges and universities have historical importance too and have been recognized as excellent centers of learning from time immemorial.

Amar Singh Government College * Location – Srinagar

* Undergraduate Courses – BA, B.Sc

Government College for Women

* Location – Gandhi Nagar

* Undergraduate Degrees – BA, B.Sc in Home Science and Vocational Courses

Government College for Boys * Location – Anantnag, Jammu and Kashmir

* Undergraduate Degrees – BA, B.Com, B.Sc

Government College of Music and Fine Arts

* Location – Srinagar

* Undergraduate Degrees – BFA (bachelor of fine arts), B.Mus (bachelor of music)

Government College Bemina

* Location – Srinagar

* Undergraduate Degrees – BA, B.Sc

* Admission Procedure – Your board results in the XIIth standard is required to seek admission to the above mentioned colleges. Admission forms are available online and from college premises.

UNIVERSITY OF KASHMIR

All colleges in Jammu and Kashmir that provide degrees in general courses in the fields of arts, science and commerce are affiliated to the University of Kashmir.

* Courses Offered – This University provides postgraduate degrees in various disciplines of science, arts and commerce. M.Ed and MCA are other degrees that several students visiting this university opt to take. After a masters degree, you can opt for higher education like M.Phil and Ph.D in the subject which you have graduated in.

* Admission Process – The graduation marks are very important to seek admission to the University level of education. There are seats reserved for students who have attended colleges under the University of Kashmir. Reservation as per government norms are followed in this university, thus there are seats reserved for scheduled tribes, scheduled castes and OBCs.

Professional Options Available in Jammu and Kashmir

Jammu and Kashmir is not only the chosen destination for

studying general courses but also for pursuing professional courses.

Today, professional curriculum has become very important because more and more people, both men and women, want to enter into a professional life as soon as possible in their lives. Therefore a professional degree is very important.

Colleges in Jammu and Kashmir

Education for Foreign Students in Jammu and Kashmir

The educational facilities and administrative infrastructure in Jammu and Kashmir is not very developed. Though studying in Jammu and Kashmir is gradually becoming the chosen option for resident students, not many international candidates travel to this Indian state for education.

Both the Central and State government authorities are trying their best to improve the scenario of education in Jammu and Kashmir. With the establishment of several schools, colleges and universities in the state, people are hopeful that foreign / NRI students will soon travel to Jammu and Kashmir not only for tourism but also for educational purposes.

However, there are reserved seats for foreign nationals in the CET (Common Entrance Test) examinations and the qualifying students can opt to study in engineering colleges of Jammu and Kashmir.

JAMMU AND KASHMIR STATE BOARD OF SCHOOL EDUCATION

The Jammu and Kashmir State Board of School Education (abbreviated as JKSBSE or JK SBOSE) is the main board of school education in the Indian state of Jammu and Kashmir. It is based in Jammu & Srinagar and is an autonomous body under the administration of the state government of Jammu and Kashmir. The board gives affiliation to more than 10200 schools across the state and employs 22856 teachers.

Purposes

According to its official website, the purposes of the board are to:

1. Secure that education should relate intimately to the development of potentialities of the youth, to the national needs and to the aspirations of the people
2. Discover talent and nurture it;
3. Promote equality of opportunity by providing necessary facilities;
4. Help generally to raise the standard of living and productivity of the State and achieve closer and willing participation of the people in a democratic process ;
5. Regulate, control and develop education in the State of Jammu and Kashmir up to the Higher Secondary level by providing varied courses with a view to equipping pupils for different occupations, for education in the universities and other cultural purposes and to examine candidates and to award certificates to successful candidates and doing all other things incidental thereto.

Composition

The Board consists of:

- The chair of the Board
- The Commissioner/ Secretary to Government School Education Department
- The Director of School Education, Jammu
- The Director of School Education, Kashmir
- A representative from each of the two Universities of Kashmir and Jammu. Each representative is appointed by Council of the University involved.
- Four school teachers, two men and two women. They are appointed by the Government. The male teachers are concerned in the education of boys, and the female teachers in that of girls.

- A well-known expert in education who is not part of the administration, but who is appointed by the Government
- A representative of the Teachers' Training Institutions. This representative is appointed by the Government.
- One man from among the Principals and Headmasters of teaching institutions in the State, appointed by the Government.
- One woman from among the Principals and Headmistress of teaching institutions in the State, appointed by the Government.

Major functions

The board is empowered to specify the courses of instruction and create syllabi for them, and to select textbooks for the elementary, and secondary schools and for the higher secondary (school gradation) school examinations; to conduct public examinations and publish the results at the secondary school and higher secondary levels; to grant diplomas or certificates to people who have passed its examinations; to recognize educational institutions at the secondary school and higher secondary levels, and conduct inspections of recognized institutions, ensuring that required facilitates, equipment, and staff are in place, that only the approved books and courses are taught, and that the standards are in accord with the relevant regulations; to remove recognition from schools that do not meet the proper conditions; to supervise and control the recognized institutions; and exercise various other powers given to it by law.

Bibliography

Alastair Lamb, Kashmir: *A Disputed Legacy 1846–1990,* Hertingfordbury, Herts: Roxford Books, 1991.

Austin, Granville: *The Indian Constitution: Cornerstone of a Nation,* Oxford, Clarendon Press, 1966.

Aziz, K. K.: *Complete Works of Mufti,* Islamabad, National Commission on Historical and Cultural Research, 1978.

Badam, G.L. and K.K. Chakravarty: *Heritage of Jammu, Kashmir and Ladakh,* Research India Press, Delhi, 2010.

Bamzai, P. N. K.: A *History of Kashmir,* Delhi: Metropolitan, 1962.

Bamzai, Prithivi Nath Kaul: *A History of Kashmir: Political, Social, Cultural.* Delhi: Metropolitan, 1962.

Buzan, Barry : *Security: A New Framework for Analysis.* Boulder: Lynne-Rienner Publishers, 1998.

Chitkara, M.G. : *Indo-Pak Relations Challenges Before New Millennium,* APH, Delhi, 2001.

Fernandes, Vivian: *Modi: Leadership, governance and Performance.* Orient Publishing. Delhi, 2014

Ghosh, Ajoy : *Indo-Pak Conflict : Threat to South Asian Security,* Reference Press, Delhi, 2003.

Ghoshal, U. N.: A *History of Indian Political Ideas.* London, 1966.

Heathcote, T. A.: *The Indian Army – The Garrison of British Imperial India, 1822–1922.* David & Charles. Newton Abbot, Devon. 1974.

Huntington, S.P.: *The Soldier and the State,* N.Y., Vintage Books, 1964.

Hussain Mushahid: *Pakistan: Problems of Governance,* Vanguard 1993.

John L. Esposito: *Islam: The Straight Path,* Oxford University Press, 1998.

Justice A.S. Anand: *The Constitution of Jammu and Kashmir.* Universal Law Publishing Co. 2006.

Kalindi Randeri: *Narendra Modi : The Architect of A Modern State*, Rupa, Delhi, 2009.

Keane J.: *Democracy and Civil Liberty in Afghanistan*, London, Verso, 1988.

Kilcullen, David: *Counterinsurgency,* Oxford University Press, 2010.

Kunju, N. : *Indo-Pak : Nuclear Cold War*, Reliance, Delhi, 2002.

Madan, Nath: *Family and Kinship: A Study of the Pandits of Rural Kashmir,* Bombay, Asia Publishing House, 1965.

Madan, Nath: *Family and Kinship: A Study of the Pandits of Rural Kashmir,* Bombay, Asia Publishing House, 1965.

Mousavi, Syed Askr: *The Hazaras of Afghanistan*. St. Martin's Press. 1997.

Mukhopadhyay, Nilanjan: *Omar: The Man, The Times*. Westkabd. 2013

Narula, Sanjay : *Ghulam and Indian Politics*, New Delhi, Murari Lal and Sons, 2007.

Nirmala Bora: *Ladakh : Society and Economy*, Anamika, Delhi, 2004.

Parvez Dewan: *A History of Jammu*, Manas, Delhi, 2008.

Pitambar Datt Kaushik: *The Congress Ideology and Programme, 1920–1985,* Gitanjali Pub. House, Delhi, 1986.

Rosen, P.: *Societies and Military Power: India and its Armies*, Ithaca, Cornell University Press, 1996.

Sardesai, Rajdeep: *2014: The Election That Changed India,* Delhi, 2014.

Seshagiri, K. L. : *Mahatma Gandhi and Comparative Religion*, Motilal Banarsidass, New Delhi, 1978.

Sumantra Bose, *The Challenge in Kashmir : democracy, self-determination and a just peace,* New Delhi: Sage, 1997.

Sumit Ganguly, *The Crisis in Kashmir,* Washington, D.C.: Woodrow Wilson Center Press; Cambridge : Cambridge U.P., 1997.

Thampi, Madhavi : *India and China in the Colonial World*, Social Science Press, Delhi, 2010.

Victoria Schofield, *Kashmir in Conflict* I.B. Tauris, London, 2005.

Wilborn, Thomas L.: *International Politics In Northeast Asia : The China-Japan-United States Strategic Triangle*. Carlisle Barracks, PA: Strategic Studies Institute, 1996.

Yasin, Mohammad : *Indian Politics : Processes, Issues and Trends,* New Delhi, Kanishka, 2004.

Index

A

Administrative Divisions, 32, 37, 51, 182.

B

Balti Language, 61.
Basket Weaving, 188.

C

Charar-e-Sharief, 156.
Constitution of Jammu and Kashmir, 33, 38, 39, 42.
Crop Combinations, 122, 123.
Cropping Patterns, 120, 121, 123, 125.
Cuisines, 14, 16.
Culture of Kashmir, 13, 157.

D

Dachigam National Park, 108, 109, 114.
Democratic Freedom Party, 54.
Democratic Janata Dal, 53.
Democratic National Conference, 53.
Directive Principles, 39, 42.
Dogri Language, 62.

E

Education System, 199.
Emergency Provisions, 42.
Energy Resources, 130.

F

Fundamental Duties, 42, 43.
Fundamental Rights, 42.

G

Government Formation, 49.
Gulmarg Biosphere, 109, 114.

H

Handicrafts, 12, 14, 17, 67, 86, 92, 122, 149, 170, 199.
Hari Parbat Fort, 24, 157.
Health Care, 133, 148.
Hydel Power, 130, 131, 132, 133.

I

Industrial Development, 141.
International Democratic Party, 53.

J

Jammu Province, 82, 97, 99, 165, 183.
Jurisdiction of Parliament, 42.

K

Kashmir Dal Lake, 160.
Kashmir Valley, 1, 12, 28, 36, 51, 56, 59, 60, 79, 83, 94, 95, 99, 107, 116, 121, 161, 167, 170, 171, 173, 175, 182, 183.
Kashmiri Language, 14, 15, 56, 59, 60, 67, 69, 77, 111.
Kashmiri Literature, 15, 57, 69, 77, 78.
Kashmiri Muslims, 13, 16, 17, 37, 183, 185.
Kashmiri Pandits, 4, 13, 16, 59, 73, 182, 183, 184, 186.

L

Laddakhi Language, 68.
Land Reforms, 124, 144.
Land Utilization, 119.
Language Spoken, 15, 60, 62, 66.
Legislative Assembly, 33, 37, 40, 43, 44, 45, 47, 48.
Lok Sabha elections, 47, 52.

M

Monuments, 22, 23, 159, 160.
Muslim Rule, 4.

O

Official Languages, 43.

P

Papier Mache, 18, 19, 188, 189, 190, 191.
Pashmina Shawls, 17, 19, 20, 187.
People of Kashmir, 48, 184.
Physical Divisions, 86, 138.
Population Density, 180.
Primary Education, 199.

R

Ramnagar Wildlife Sanctuary, 109.
Rural Electrification, 132.

S

Separatist Insurgency, 34.
Shina Language, 68.
Social Welfare, 148.

T

Textile Works, 190.

V

Vaishno Devi, 154, 155, 156, 165, 170, 171, 173, 174, 175, 178, 198.

W

Wood Carvings, 191.

❑❑❑

www.ingramcontent.com/pod-product-compliance
Ingram Content Group UK Ltd.
Pitfield, Milton Keynes, MK11 3LW, UK
UKHW042016290726
14061UKWH00001BB/24